AN OLD CRACKED CUP

AN OLD CRACKED CUP

by
Margaret Rorke

NORTHWOOD INSTITUTE PRESS
Midland, Michigan 48640

First Edition

© 1980 by Northwood Institute Press

LCN 80-84326   ISBN 0-87359-023-6

Printed in the United States of America

DEDICATION

To the Glory of God and to the Memory of My Bill,
(William Craig Rorke) who now resides with Him.

"To have lived with love is to have lived." I have lived! The many of you who have read "My Ego Trip" have some idea of just how happy that period was. I am deeply thankful for it.

I would like to mention all of the friends whose support, affection and encouragement I cherish, but I refrain from putting names in black and white for fear of inadvertently missing someone important. You out there know who you are. Please drink deeply of my gratitude.

CONTENTS & TITLE INDEX

FOREWORD

The years fade away and it is difficult to account for them, so let's just say it was about a decade ago when Margaret Rorke's first poem arrived at my desk. I was holding forth in the Detroit Free Press building at the time, and writing six columns a week, so contributions from readers were treated with tender loving care.

But poetry? It is no violation of guild secrets to say that a columnist would rather receive a threatening letter from a lawyer than a bit of verse from a subscriber. There are several reasons for this aversion, the cardinal one being that if it has merit, and you print it, you immediately attract a slew of offerings which are not quite so enchanting. It is amazing how many closet poets there are in this land, all anxious to see their work in print. You feel for them, you love them each and every one, you understand their frustrations, but what they add up to is a no-win situation, for in pleasing one you offend a dozen others, and there is little profit in that.

There are, however, exceptions to almost every rule, and Margaret Rorke's work is a sterling example. She had (I later learned) been writing and publishing for a number of years, and the economy and clarity of her style made an instant and lasting impression on those who turn to my place in the paper. There have been innumerable letters and comments praising her contributions, and many columns have been "written around" the moods she created. She has been, in short, a jewel—and it is an honor to participate in this presentation of "An Old Cracked Cup".

When Margaret Rorke writes a poem, the reader does not have to walk around for an hour or two with hand clasped to forehead, asking: "What is she trying to say? What did she mean by that?" She is not devious; she does not travel by circuitous route; she leaves no stray pennants flapping in an uncertain breeze. Instead, she sets the theme, develops it with charm and grace, and you follow her to a substantial conclusion, sorry it ended so soon.

I am highly partial to what Margaret Rorke stands for in love and concern for humanity and where we are headed, God help us all. "An Old Cracked Cup" is timely to a nation that, in some instances, seems to have lost its way. It is hoped that hundreds of readers will find in it substantial traces of the road back.

Judd Arnett

Howell, Michigan
October, 1980

A CUP OF SUN

An old cracked cup sat on the stair
For I forgot and left it there.
A shaft of sunlight filled its bowl
And warmed what would have been a hole.

How much like me—that old cracked cup—
Made happy by what fills it up.
For me, it's warmth that comes from love
And rays of faith from up above.

Intangible these fillers be:
The cup's full glow, the midst of me;
And, yet, when all is said and done,
Life's finest is its cup of sun.

ABOVE ALL

Above the world of ancient trade
Where clumsy camels chewed and swayed
And plopped their padded feet;
Above the burdens on their backs,
The merchandise in saddle-packs,
Above the business beat,
There shone a Star.

Above the Roman soldier's head,
Above down-trodden looks of dread
At helmet, shield and spear;
Above the chariots of brass
Where rumbling rode the wealthy class;
Above the social sphere,
There shone a Star.

Above the same old world today,
The light that shows the better way
To fill our mortal cup
Still glows as in those days of old.
Oh, may our hearts by love be told
We'll see if we look up
There shines a Star.

ADMISSION FREE

The scene is lit with amber light—
    The sun's soft golden glow.
Chrysanthemums and asters bright
    Are footlights from below.
Beyond them stands the world of trees
    In every painted hue . . .
A set that's very sure to please
    Right from the starting cue.

A squirrel scurries 'cross the stage
    To take its purposed place.
A wedge of geese, divinely sage,
    Checks off its flying space.
The sky inhales to let it pass
    Without a lasting mark;
Then gazes into lake-made glass
    To catch its azure arc.

The wind with many whiney throats,
    Like tuning violins
Perfecting their orchestral notes
    Before the play begins,
Prepares to sound the op'ning score.
    The curtain time is now.
Let us applaud as ne'er before
    As Autumn takes her bow.

... AND IT CAME TO PASS

And it came to pass in those days of old—
Yes, it came to pass as it was foretold,
That the Town of David drew in its clan,
And a girl, fifteen, rode beside her man
On a weary trip for one great with child.
Other trav'llers marveled that still she smiled.

And it came to pass that this lad, nineteen,
Who pursued a carpenter's trade and mien
In a land where wood was as scarce as meat
Should be called to Bethlehem's dusty street
In the Roman records to be enrolled.
Yes, it came to pass—as it's now retold.

And that night the inn was reported full,
And these two who came had no power—no "pull"
To obtain a bed for a restful night;
But the keeper noted the young girl's plight,
And he showed the couple a cave he kept
Where the animals and the asses slept.

There the grateful pair from the world withdrew.
All alone they faced what they had to do.
He prepared a stall with some manger straw,
Built a fire outside that no others saw,
Heated water, waited, and softly prayed
Till the newborn cry of a babe was made.

(Continued on next page)

Then she called. He came. There in swaddling clothes
Lay the infant Christ, red of cheek and nose—
The Messiah, born as the angel said.
And the Wise Men knew, for they all had read
The prophetic lines in the books of old;
So they left with incense and myrrh and gold.

And it came to pass that those tending ewes
Were the first informed of the great glad news—
Of the Savior born to bring peace—good will
To a frightened world—as that world is still.
But the Way was born to a humble lass,
And to all who help it to come to pass.

ANNUAL MEETING INVOCATION

Dear Lord,

> Our year now ends. Our year begins—
> Much as the globe of seasons spins
>   With undetected seam.
> From those whose terms are now fulfilled,
> We take a legacy to build
>   Upon the future's dream.
>
> Help those who've led us in the past
> To know our thankfulness will last.
>   Bless those about to guide
> With thoughts that nourish as this food,
> For which we give our gratitude—
>   And with their goals abide.

Amen.

APRIL

They call their baby "April."
　　Oh, what a lovely name!
It conjures up a picture
　　Too free to fit a frame:

A dainty little blossom—
　　A tiny crocus bud—
That pushes past dissuasion
　　To part the melting mud;

A timid, furry bunny,
　　A yellow-feathered chick,
A glimpse of green transfusing
　　What had appeared a stick;

A robin brightly breasted
　　A-singing to the sky
As if to ask for color
　　To use for eggshell dye;

A branch of pussy willow,
　　A brook with babbling tongue,
A lambkin in a meadow:
　　Just all that's fresh and young.

They call their baby "April"—
　　The month of hope and cheer.
How nice to carry "April"
　　Around with one all year!

AS DAY BEGINS

Dear Lord,
I thank You for the gift of day,
   Refreshed by last night's rest:
Another chance to do and say
   What's hopefully my best.

Allow me to pursue my tasks
   With vigor and with joy,
Ignoring what impatience asks
   Or fretful moods employ.

Let thinking seek a higher goal
   Than pity for what's me
Or anger at another's role
   Whose motives I can't see.

Keep ever foremost in my mind
   'Tis You I need so much,
And You're around for me to find
   If I'll just keep in touch.

Genesis 1:3-5   And God said, "Let there be light"; and
there was light. And God saw that the light
was good; and God separated the light
from the darkness. God called the light
Day, and the darkness Night.

Psalms 145:18   The Lord is near to all who call upon him,
to all who call upon him in truth.

AS WE MEET

God, bless us as we bow our heads
    And kneel our loving thought.
Behold the path our purpose treads
    For which Your lead is sought.
Upon the altar of our hearts
    We place our faith in You,
And, as our purposed meeting starts,
    Please sanction what we do.

Help each put thought of self aside
    To unify our goal,
But help each feel he can provide
    His portion of the whole.
For we are met for strength to do
    What none can do alone.
We pray our aims are pleasing You
    As if they were Your own.

AUGUST

Augie's the month in the tattered straw hat,
Off with a fish pole and puppy to pat,
Whistling along—fully freckled and tan—
Still more a youngster than he is a man.

Augie is chawing on apples and pears,
Taking his produce to big county fairs,
Plumping himself with the earth's yellow yields.
Corn fills his tummy, and wheat fills his fields.

Augie's contented with life in the sun—
Robust and given to rollicking fun—
Just a bit rustic, but surely no fool:
Augie will leave just in time to miss school.

BEAUTY IS FOREVER

Beauty is forever
    If it lies beneath the skin.
Time can't reach to sever
    That which blossoms from within.

Cheeks may crack belying
    All the decades drifted by;
But there's no denying
    What still sparkles in the eye.

When the ore is tested
    By the flames of love and trust,
Where it long has rested,
    It rebuts the surface rust.

There can be no fading
    Of a pattern wrapped by years
To withstand invading
    By a multitude of fears.

Beauty is forever,
    Given what should be its role.
Age is not so clever
    As to wrinkle up the soul.

BEAUTY OBSCURED

Dear God, If on a given day
My outlook should be drear and gray,
Lift me above those murky mists
To see the beauty that exists.

Life's situations may seem grim—
Solutions difficult and dim,
And other people hard to bear,
But keep me mindful beauty's there.

Oh, strengthen me to brush aside
Whatever makes that beauty hide
Behind a veil that's snagged and caught
On some small hurt or petty thought.

Then help me with Your peace divine—
As polish—make that beauty shine
'Til its reflection let's You see
A bit of beauty, God, in me.

Psalms 27:4   "One thing I desired of the Lord, that will
I seek after . . . to behold the beauty of
the Lord."

BEFORE THE SLUMP

I never knew my husband
    Had a figure quite so trim.
I felt a bit chagrined that
    I had failed to notice him.
For there, just like Apollo,
    Stood the man whom I had wed . . .
His chest expanded fully
    Like I'd never seen it spread.
Erect he seemed to tower
    All the beings I had known.
His back was like an arrow:
    Straight and strong and stiff of bone.
His middle was much flatter
    Than I ever could recall.
In fact, on close inspection,
    I could find no bulge at all.
He surely was attractive
    In the shades of grey and blue.
It really didn't matter
    For he flattered every hue.
Then something set me musing
    On the truth I can't refute:
Too bad he takes to breathing
    When at last he's bought a suit.

FOR BEING GOD

We thank you, God, for being God,
    In this our grateful prayer,
For making ours the pilgrim sod,
    The virgin nation where
The soil produces fruit and grain
    For body, mind and soul,
And freedom labors to sustain
    Its life in every goal.

We thank you, God, for all that's ours,
    For family and friends,
For guiding us by unseen powers
    Toward all productive ends,
For patience, comfort, joy and love,
    For which all mortals yearn:
For being God—all else above!
    If not, where could we turn?

BETHLEHEM BOUND

Bethlehem bound on the road that day
Journeyed the folks with a tax to pay.
Rome had decreed that it be that way.

Bethlehem bound 'mong the milling mass
Traveled a pair that the proud would pass,
Joseph and Mary upon an ass.

Bethlehem bound on that Holy Night
Wisemen rode on with His sign for light,
Certain they'd come to a wond'rous sight.

Bethlehem bound with but love to bring
Shepherds who'd harkened to angels sing
Started through fields to behold their King.

Bethlehem bound on this Christmas Eve
Pilgrim all folks who in faith believe,
Looking for Him whom their hearts receive.

Bethlehem bound for the world's release,
Praying that wars on this earth may cease,
Man still is seeking the Prince of Peace.

BEWITCHING

Masking her childhood on Halloween,
Sweet baby features were painted mean.
Dwarfed without potion, this ugly hag
Stood at my door with her open bag.
Slightly recoiling to feign my fear
Loosened a smile from the little dear—
Making her lips an elliptical wreath
Baring the absence of two front teeth.
This, you'll admit, was an ill-timed sight,
Causing her fierceness to lose its bite.

BIRTHDAY GIFTS

Youth sees candles on a cake
    Few enough to blow.
Vast the future still at stake!
    Brief the afterglow!
Toys and trinkets are the gifts
    Young folks understand,
But the hourglass faster sifts
    Year by year its sand.

Age must greet its natal day
    As, itself, the prize:
One more year that's stowed away
    Goods that good supplies—
Best of fam'ly, best of friends
    Bless the inner eye:
Gifts on which the heart depends
    For its love supply.

BLESS OUR BEST

Oh, Lord of all earth's lovely things . . .
The ones that fly on colored wings . . .
The variegated ones that grow . . .
The blue of waters . . . white of snow . . .
The soil You've shaped so many ways . . .
And "seasoned" always to amaze:
For all of these accept our praise.

Oh, Lord of life in all its forms . . .
Its sun . . . its moon . . . its stars . . . its storms . . .
Its creatures, be they large or small,
And us . . . You love the most of all,
Behold and bless our noble ends:
Pursuit of knowledge, quest of friends . . .
And faith on which it all depends.

Amen.

THE BLIGHTED BUD

'Mong the roses on the table
    That were cut to grace the room,
There was one, though fully able,
    Which refused to open bloom.
It remained a blighted buddling
    With its petals snugly tight,
As though each to each was huddling
    From the summons of the light.

It refused to give its beauty
    Ere the life within it sped.
It declined to do its duty.
    It preferred to hang its head.
What could make it such a quitter?
    Did it pout 'cause it was cut?
Did a vase-mate make it bitter
    So it sealed its blessings shut?

What a waste of fragrant magic!
    What a loss to the bouquet!
But the end was far more tragic
    For the bud that fell away
Never knowing its potential,
    For it never felt the pull
Of the Power so essential
    To its living to the full.

BREAD BAIT

I telephoned to Bill and said
That I would like a loaf of bread.
He told me he would write a note,
And pin it to his overcoat.

When supper time at last arrived,
I knew with someone he'd connived.
Above the sacks I saw his hat.
His arms were just as full as that.

As groc'ries filled the cupboard top,
He said, "My dear, I couldn't stop.
You know, I've never tried this cheese,
And here's the newest thing they freeze."

"This bottle just looked awf'lly nice,
And of this meat I bought a slice.
They say these crackers just came in,
And now they pack this stuff in tin."

The grocer has a clever trap.
He puts his foods in tempting wrap,
And on his counters they are spread
To catch the man who comes for bread.

BUTTERFLY KISSES

Butterfly kisses! I almost forgot!
    Really that would have been bad.
Watching a mother a-hugging her tot
    Posted a mem'ry I had.
Long, long ago, I was given that treat—
    One that a child shouldn't miss.
Often I stood on the toes of my feet
    Just for a butterfly kiss.

Butterfly kiss—don't you know how it's done?
    Gather a cheek to your eye.
Brush it with "winkers" you flutter in fun.
    Soon it will giggle and cry,
"Oh, how it tickles, let's do it again!
    Do it to sister like this!"
Tell me, though, mother, just where and just when
    You saw a butterfly kiss?

Mothers don't see them, and yet mothers know—
    Know that it has to be true
Just 'cause the mother they loved told them so.
    That's how I know it. Don't you?
Maybe a butterfly settled on Eve
    Back when all Eden was bliss,
Showing her how; so all tykes might receive
    Joys of a butterfly kiss.

THE CALL

In the midst of the fray
When the bad man's at bay,
And the posse is springing the trap,
There's the call all can hear,
And its order is clear:
It is time for the bad man to nap!

When the wagons and trikes
And the scooters and bikes
In the drive are a jumbled-up bunch,
And the cop with his shout
Tries to straighten them out,
There's the call for the cop to have lunch.

When the bases are filled,
And the game could be spilled
Or be won by the fellow at bat,
There is worry, it seems,
On the part of both teams;
For the call chooses moments like that.

THE CARPENTER'S CALL

He followed the call
    of the carpenter's trade.
Though no one has told us
    the things that He made,
We'd guess they were cradles
    and tables and chairs—
The items then listed
    as carpenters' wares.

We'd guess that the homes
    where the humble folks dwelled
Were braced by the beams
    that The Carpenter felled.
We'd guess He was skillful
    with hammer and awl
And faithfully answered
    the carpenter's call.

We'd guess all of this
    for we cannot ignore
That Christ with His living
    constructed a door
And carved on its face
    how His fellows should live—
Should love, should be faithful,
    should help and forgive.

He finished that door
    with the nails in His hands.
It opened to Him
    all the Heavenly Lands.
He left it ajar
    with its promise for all
That morning The Carpenter
    answered His call.

THE CART AHEAD

I know he came to the groc'ry store
    For frankfurters, beans and bread.
He didn't mean to depart with more.
    'Twas clear from the list he read.

But once inside I could see him pause
    Near rose bushes burlap-wrapped.
He didn't stop very long because
    He suddenly felt entrapped.

He picked up one and was on his way
    With frankfurters, beans and bread.
I learned a lot 'bout that man today,
    And how he, indeed, is fed.

CAT AND GHOST

I looked outside into the night.
    'Twas dark as ebon peat.
Then, Lo! I saw in fullest flight
    Some mother's snowy sheet.
I might have wilted at the sight,
    But 'neath its folds were feet.

It waited just beneath the tree
    That guards yon neighbor's door.
It wasn't long ere I could see
    Just what it waited for . . .
A big black cat down on one knee
    Whose shoe lace was a chore.

Then hand in hand the cat and ghost
    Gave forth a warning shout
To him prepared to be a host
    To every neighbor's sprout.
With open bags they gleaned the most
    Before they turned about.

In time the porchlights lost their stare
    All up and down the street
As cupboards fast were growing bare
    Of things for tramps to eat.
I turned to see upon a chair
    A cat's head and a sheet.

24

THE CATCH

Putting salt on his tail—
    You all doubtless have heard—
Is the way without fail
    For obtaining a bird.
It has often been tried
    For the method is old,
And a youngster wide-eyed
    Can be easily sold.

When the robins return
    In the season of spring,
Little children all yearn
    To caress a soft wing;
So they hastily run
    Where a redbreast may be,
But he ends all their fun
    By his flight to a tree.

It is then that we say,
    With a tongue in our cheek,
That we know of a way
    They can have what they seek,
And our words so profound
    They accept without fault
As they're kitchen-ward bound
    For a shaker of salt.

Is the trick really fair?
    Should we pass it on thus
Just because we're aware
    It was once played on us?
I'm not certain as yet
    It's unworthy of sale
For no man have I met
    Who has salted a tail!

A LITTLE CHILD

Unsteady the feet
That toddle to meet
And to be with the
    objects of love.
With eyes straight ahead
The body is led
To depend on a
    hand from above.

A face, pure in smile,
That thought can't defile;
For thinking as yet
    has no chart
To envy or greed.
It seeks but to feed
On the wonders
    each day may impart.

As little hands reach
Toward those who would teach,
Oh, what trust
    in the untainted soul!
What model, indeed,
For grown-ups to heed!
What a difficult way
    to God's goal!

Matthew 18:2

CHRISTMASTIME IS HERE

All is hustle-bustle,
    Feel it in the air?
Hear the tissue rustle,
    Crushed to cloak with care
Something as a token
    For a person dear,
Wrapping love unspoken.
    Christmastime is here.

See the tinsel glisten,
    Hear the sound of bells;
Pause a bit and listen,
    Nothing else excels.
Joy is in suspension.
    Hark the carols clear
Taking turns to mention
    Christmastime is here.

Note the light aglowing
    In a youngster's eyes.
There's no way of knowing
    How to price that prize.
Candles fade beside it.
    It illumes the sphere.
There's no way to hide it . . .
    Christmastime is here.

Fellowfolk are kinder,
    We are kinder, too;
Each a would-be finder
    Of some good to do.
This, the grand sensation,
    Rises once a year
With the realization
    Christmastime is here.

AFTER CHRISTMAS

When the star of that night
Had been blotted from sight,
When the song of the Angel was still,
When the little town woke
'Neath the harsh Roman yoke,
And the shepherds were back on the hill;
Nothing really had changed.
Life was not rearranged.
Man went on with his toil and his trade,
For but few really knew
What that Baby would do.
Little diff'rence that first Christmas made.

But each year as we go
To the manger, we know
The true meaning of all that we see.
Wiser wisdom we hold
Than the wise men of old.
Time has proven that Baby was He,
Son of God, Son of Man
Sent to offer God's plan,
Sent to live, sent to teach, sent to die
That we'd seek greater worth
For ourselves and our earth.
Oh, may knowing all this, help us try!

THE AGES OF CHRISTMAS

It isn't just a special day
 That thrills us once a year.
Each adds to each in such a way
 That each becomes more dear.
The little child so bright of eye,
 Surrounded by earth's love,
Imagines Santa riding by
 Beneath the Star above.
His parents see God's gift to earth
 As wisemen saw the soul.
They know the miracle of birth.
 They've cherished Mary's role.
The folks to whom long mem'ries bring
 What shepherd hearts can't scorn
Rejoice to hear the angels sing,
 "A Savior is born!"

CHRISTMAS DAY

Over hatred and dark
There descended a Star,
Giving love a new spark,
Sending light near and far,
Making old wisdom fresh,
Causing shepherds' dismay . . .
As the "Word was made flesh"
On that first Christmas Day.

It still shines. Let it lead
To the manger once more
Where His love fills your need.
See His light at the door!
Let your heart hold the creche
In the tenderest way
For the "Word is made flesh"
Every year—Christmas Day.

CHRISTMAS GREETING

May your Christmas be merry
    the whole day through.
May the spirit of Santa
    be good to you.
May the legends of holly
    and mistletoe
Take their root in your
    life and forever grow.

May you travel once more
    into David's town.
At the stable's approach
    lay your burdens down
While you enter and kneel
    as the shepherds knelt,
While you feel in your heart
    what the wisemen felt.

May you see as a shadow
    because of Him
All that blackens your daylight
    or makes it dim.
May your friends and your faith
    have that strength divine
With which God, as a symbol,
    has graced the pine.

May you hear in the echoes
    the angel band
Sing of Peace and Good Will
    over all our land.
If our Father will make
    what I wish come true,
Christmas Day will be merry
    for yours and you.

ONE CHRISTMAS MORNING

In the morning I met with a "shepherd",
    With a soul like the ones tending sheep,
One content to be caring for others
    With no thought of the glory he'd reap.

Then I listened a while to a "wiseman"
    To whose wisdom I only could nod,
For his learning had reached such a summit
    That he spoke very simply of God.

Oh, the morning, the morning of Chirstmas,
    I'd experienced what couldn't be priced.
I had talked with two wonderful people
    Who had been to the cradle of Christ.

CHRISTMAS PARALLELS

In an overcrowded section
    Of a city unconcerned,
In the midst of man's rejection,
    Was a stable, so we've learned,
Where was born the little Baby,
    Wrapped in simple swaddling clothes.
Of this fact there is no "maybe",
    As a faithful Christian knows.

Those were days of crime and riot.
    There were thieves on every road,
And it was with some disquiet
    Man went forth from his abode.
Those were days of great oppression.
    Rome was ruthless in its rule.
Yet this period of transgression
    Was the setting for our Yule.

There were taxes much too heavy
    For the people then to pay,
And enrollment for one levy
    Made our Savior sleep on hay.
There were wars. There was confusion.
    There was trouble with the youth.
There was need for an infusion
    In some form of love and truth.

There was poverty and power.
    There was hatred, Herod-style,
That would use God's promised hour
    To destroy the most worthwhile.
'Twas a period far from pleasant.
    Burdened people sought release.
And for them as for the present
    There was born the Prince of Peace.

CHRISTMAS SOUNDS

Listen to the angels!
    Their song is with us still.
It ever circles 'round us
    And echoes "Peace—Good Will".

Is that a tinkling sleighbell?
    No . . . camel bells we hear.
Wisemen still cross deserts
    To find what God makes clear.

Shepherd sandals shuffle
    While starlight reigns above.
Hark! a mother's singing
    Her lullaby of love.

All these sounds are with us.
    They ever gird the earth.
Listen! In your heartbeat,
    You'll hear His cry at birth.

CHURCH PRAYER

Dear God,

From every walk of life we come
    To this, Your house, today,
The weak, the worn, the wearisome,
    The glad, the grieved, the gay.
Community in miniature
    By faith on Sunday led
Into Your presence, perfect, pure
    To have its spirit fed.

We come each week to share an hour
    In fellowship with man,
Together seeking here the power
    To carry out Your plan
For all of us—for each of us.
    We open here our hearts
To hold the soul-sent stimulus
    This solemn hour imparts.

Oh, make us not a passive crowd
    Who hears Your message read
And sings the hymns with voice aloud
    And prays with lowered head,
But leaves Your house the way it came—
    No better and no worse.
God, spark in us a fervid flame
    To light the universe.

CHURCH CIRCLE PRAYER

Father:

We who gather in this circle
    In the name of Him, our Lord,
Are like single bits of driftwood
    Strung together on a cord.
It's the cord we have in common.
    It's the cord that makes us strong;
For the cord is faith in Jesus
    And His church where we belong.

In this circle, friend and neighbor
    Meet to further Christian worth,
Meet to give of time and labor
    For the betterment of earth . . .
And this little plot around us
    Where we make our biggest dent . . .
Lord, in looking, may You find us
    Well achieving Your intent.

THE CHURCH HOUR

Dear God,

Into Your house we come today
To hear Your Word, to sing and pray;
To seek a refuge for the soul
Beyond the outer world's control . . .
    For just an hour.

Before Your altar, problems kneel,
Remorse and grief make their appeal;
While joy and triumph close their ranks
To offer up their earnest thanks
    For just an hour.

So little time provides so much,
As we submit to feel Your touch—
Your love-directed peace of mind.
What great exchange is ours to find
    For just an hour!

OUR CHURCH

Our church is its ministers through the years
Who've fostered the faith that defeats our fears,
Who've comforted, counseled and led this flock,
Our personal "Peters"—each one, a "rock".

Our church is its organists, those who quote
The scripture as sung with a pipey throat.
Our church is its choirs, where the gifted voice
So fills list'ning souls that they must rejoice.

Our church is a babe in baptismal dress
Symbolically named for the Lord to bless.
Our church is its youth in a pastor's class,
Receiving the Bible the day they pass.

Our church is its children in Sunday School
Where mischief oft vies with the Golden Rule.
Our church is its teachers who give their time
As though they were tapped by the Will Sublime.

Our church is its boards and its staffs—those parts
Computer exact, but with human hearts.
Our church is its circles, its groups who pray,
Who study and work for the Christian way.

Our church is all us on the day of days
Who meet in God's House in a mood of praise.
This thought I believe has been underscored:
Our church is its people! Oh, bless them, Lord!

THE CLOSEST COOKIE

I began to talk of manners
    And the one I'd advocate
With particular attention
    To a certain cookie plate
That I just had finished passing.
    What was once a stately stack
With dispatch became the vestige
    Of a juvenile attack.

"It's polite to take the closest
    As the cookies come around
With no eye to size or raisins"
    Was my lesson most profound
For the little group of munchers,
    And I feared it made no hit
'Til one asked, "Is it politeness
    If we turn the plate a bit?"

Now, an etiquette compiler
    Would deny the course he sought,
But beyond the flush of humor
    Lies a philosophic thought:
Few of us accept the meager
    As we take the dish of Fate.
If the better lies beyond us,
    We attempt to turn the plate.

THE COLD SNAP

The old North Wind inhaled for weeks
And then let full, distended cheeks
Emit a blast of frosty air
Across the landscape everywhere.
His breath made brittle all the trees.
The birds inflated 'gainst the breeze.
Man closer drew his thoughts and coat,
Rejecting regions more remote,
As snow was heard to crunch and squeal
Beneath the weight of foot and wheel.
The old North Wind's not mean or bold—
He simply caught himself a cold.

TO COMFORT YOU

What can I say to comfort you?
    No mortal has the word.
One but repeats God's promise true
    Which twelve disciples heard.

What sympathy is mine to give?
    I point to Easter Day—
The proof that love will always live
    Though parted 'long the way.

What thoughts of solace can I bring
    To lift your clouds of gloom?
I bid you hear the songbirds sing
    And see the tulips bloom.

What can I do to ease that grief
    From which no mortal's spared,
But hope you hold in firm belief
    The faith so lately shared?

As you will note, I but review
    What time has underscored:
The only comfort I give you
    Is comfort from the Lord.

A COMMON CALLING

I heard her calling, "Mildred"
   In accents loud and clear—
This not too distant neighbor,
   But Mildred didn't hear.
Again the name repeated,
   More urgent than before;
But, when there was no answer,
   I heard her voice implore,
"Here! Kitty, kitty, kitty!"

Then came a little tinkle
   Across the nearby street.
I judged that it was Mildred
   On four a-flying feet.
There's something 'bout the rhythm,
   Regardless of the name,
One universal summons
   Invites all cats the same:
"Here! Kitty, kitty, kitty!"

COMMUNION PRAYER

It wasn't for the twelve alone
    You broke symbolic bread,
For all of us to whom You're known
    Have ever since been fed
The body of the Christian creed
    You suffered so to give.
Oh, bless this morsel that we need
    So better we may live.

It wasn't for the twelve alone
    You passed the Holy Cup,
For we who call Your way our own
    Are too allowed to sup
The blood that strengthens and sustains
    The more that it is used.
Oh, bless this token that our veins
    May truly be transfused.

It wasn't for the twelve alone
    You met for just one night.
You meet with all where love is shown,
    Where folks would do what's right,
Where they are met to praise and pray
    And seek Your proffered aid.
Oh, whisper to our hearts today
    And keep them unafraid.

CONFLICT OF LAWS

"No Tresspassing" the sign decreed.
Don't enter here whate'er your need—
Observe the pale of yonder gate:
All this it seemed to bluntly state.
It kept me out but not my gaze
That watched infraction's many ways:
A flock of gulls that couldn't read
Swooped down to rest a bit and feed.
A wily squirrel just flicked his tail.
It threatened him to no avail.
I wondered what enforcement plan
Had been conceived by mortal man,
And how he'd sentence . . . how he'd fine
A jay for sitting on the sign.

COUNTING TO THREE

I heard an expression, nostalgic in tone.
It took me back ages to tykes of my own.
To one with a temper and lungs on a spree,
His father informed him, "I'm counting to three."

A "counting to three", I am willing to bet
Was thought up by Adam to use as a threat.
There's time between numbers when tensions dismount,
And rare is the father who's finished the count.

What happens at "three"? How can anyone tell?
Oh, would that world crises were handled as well!
Just think of the peace and the progress there'd be
If blessed with the outcome of counting to three.

45

MY DAILY PRAYER

Dear God, In faith I come to Thee
   Through Your beloved Son.
The way He taught that it should be,
   My daily prayer's begun.

You read upon my open soul
   The things for which I long.
If they're consistent with Your goal,
   Then make my purpose strong.

If they're denied, don't leave me blind,
   The prey of inner strife;
But help me ever seek to find
   The way, the truth, the life.

Lead me away from self concern,
   From pettiness and sham,
Reminding me at every turn
   Because You are, I am.

DANDELIONS

Yellow buttons dot the lawn—
Sprinkled there last night!
Nothing could so quickly spawn
Fully blown and bright.
Random tossed as if mere tots
Dropped them toddling 'round,
Smiling sunward all these spots
Fasten down the ground.

DARK AND DOUBT

Around the cross stand dark and doubt
To watch the life of light ebb out.
They have the power to quench the spark,
Those men whose knowledge is the dark.
They have the fears which force the deed
For doubt makes up their only creed,
But He with faith to see Him through
Knows well "they know not what they do".

Though Pilate finds no fault in Him,
He worries 'bout a Caesar's whim.
The mob who knows how Romans rule
Thinks Him a weak and stupid fool.
In dark and doubt they cannot know
The spark they snuff will leave a glow
To light a faith forever new.
Christ says, "They know not what they do!"

The world-accusing clouds of night
Close in to curtain Him from sight.
The temple veil is rent in twain
As God delivers Him from pain.
His mortal life so just and good
By dark and doubt misunderstood
Is closed for ages hence to view
By them who "know not what they do."

DAWN

At dawn on that first Easter Day,
An angel rolled the stone away
    And waited for the three
Who came with trembling fear and dread
To lovingly anoint the Dead,
    But dawn had found Him free.

That dawn's great resurrection light
Awakened those who had the sight
    To see His truth revealed.
They grasped the answer granted grief.
They sensed the power of belief.
    All this the dawn unsealed.

That dawn there was a great rebirth
Of what would make a better earth
    According to God's plan.
May we this Easter Day awake
With resurrected zeal to make
    A brighter dawn for man.

DEAR SANTA

Last night I wrote to Santa Claus.
    Before he closed his pack,
I thought I'd better write because
    Of many things I lack.

I asked him for a train of thought
    To climb life's higher hill
And stop at stations, Should and Ought,
    To take in firmer will.

I asked him for a spirit strong
    Enough to never break,
To well withstand both fear and wrong
    And bumps it has to take.

I asked him for a faithful heart—
    The kind one winds with prayer—
That leaps with each repeated start
    Because God's hand is there.

I asked him for life's finest sweets—
    A sugar-coated year—
One filled with gay, assorted treats
    In tier on endless tier.

Before I mailed my letter out,
    I penned a postscript too
And asked him as he went about
    To bring like gifts to you.

DECEMBER

The year's dying ember
Of course, is December.
    In sleep little creatures are curled;
But, just as it's ending,
One spark all transcending
    Flares up with a warmth for the world.

The trees get no barer—
The fields—never sparer;
    But life keeps its promise ajar.
Our loved ones seem dearer
As cold skies grow clearer
    To show us the path of the Star.

DIVINELY HUMAN

Divinely human, Christ was born
    To Mary in a cave.
The Son of God his natal morn—
    The Jesus sent to save—
Was but a babe to shepherds' view
    When He arrived on earth;
Yet so divine that wisemen knew
    Of His prophetic worth.

Divinely human, Jesus walked
    With those who shared His day.
The parables in which He talked—
    The miracles—convey
The spark divine within His power;
    Yet human was His touch.
This blend in that despotic hour
    The world was needing much.

Divinely human, too, alas,
    His blood was seen to spill.
The man who wished the cup to pass
    Divinely sought God's will.
His human death, His skill divine
    To show His promise true
Prove other lives—like yours and mine—
    Divinely human too.

DIVINITY DUST

Something makes earth a much
        friendlier sphere
As it rolls 'round to this time
        of the year.
I like to think that His star
        from its crust
Drops just a bit of divinity dust.

Something besparkles the eyes of
        a child.
Something curves lips that but
        rarely have smiled.
Something inspires greater love—
        greater trust.
Couldn't it be some divinity dust?

Voices are sweeter—now lifted
        in song.
More is perfection, and far less
        is wrong.
People draw nearer what's good
        and what's just,
Sprinkled, I'm sure, with divinity
        dust.

Glorious globe that announced
        He was born,
Come close to those who are
        sad or forlorn,
Give to their lives what I think
        is a must.
Powder them well with divinity
        dust.

THE DOOR THAT STICKS

Our house has lived our married life;
For we were newly man and wife
When we acquired our little nest.
For thirty years it has been blessed
With all the colors time can mix.
It's also had a door that sticks.

When all is done and all is said,
A handy man I did not wed.
He's good about most household rules,
Unless, of course, they call for tools.
And that is why his fam'ly kicks
The bottom of the door that sticks.

Sometimes I feel there's been a feud—
"At six and sevens" sort of mood—
Between that barrier of wood
And us whose egress it's withstood . . .
Til now respect forbids we fix—
Just gently curse—the door that sticks.

WHEN DOWN-HEARTED

Dear God, Lift up my sagging soul.
    Give breath to what You see
Until the spirit's full and whole
    In what comprises "me".

Lift off the downside of today:
    Its worry and its care,
And let me think in such a way
    That all seems sweet and fair.

My mind can burden what I do,
    Can weigh with such a load
Or churn with pictures—oft untrue—
    Or fears I can't decode.

I waste Your time. I waste my own—
    In conjurings of wrong.
Lift up my soul. Remove its stone
    Replacing it with song.

DREAMER and DOER

God, bless the dreamer,
    the one with his scope
Fixed on an image
    that's haloed by hope,
Seeing life's visible
    methods and means
Clearly portrayed by
    invisible scenes.

God, bless the doer
    who translates the view
Into reality—borning
    the new,
Braving his drudgery,
    hour after hour.
Show him his purpose,
    potential and power.

Dreamer and doer,
    the ultimate blend
Needed for every
    conceivable end!
God, bless their union,
    their fusion for growth,
You, who from wisdom
    created them both.

EARLY FRIENDSHIPS

Our early friendships never fade,
    Nor do they split from wear.
The threads from which these bonds are made
    Are memories we share.

Those memories contain a strength
    Akin to strength of youth
That, as the years increase in length,
    Intensifies this truth.

Much sharper to the aging eye
    Are trials a long time spent.
Much clearer are the days gone by
    With laughter lightly lent

Than what is going on right now
    When problems posed are real;
And time's too hurried to allow
    The furrowed brow to feel.

We may not meet or clasp the hand
    Or even ply the pen,
But still we're sure folks understand
    Who knew us way back when . . .

Because there pulls a tighter tie
    To old friends than to new;
And they'll agree and tell you why:
    They share those mem'ries too.

EARLY SNOW

The flakes are falling one by one
And twirling in a mood of fun.
    These fragile, frothy spots
Dance on as though in dancing class,
And, 'gainst the pines or still green grass
    Are nature's "polka" dots.

EASTER

As summoned by an unseen nod,
New life is surging through the sod,
    And hope revives the heart.
Earth whispers with its warming breath,
"Behold the proof! There is no death.
    Its vestiges depart."

The feathered folk their anthems sing
To praise the miracles of spring,
    Reminding us this hour
Where rests the glory of God's plan,
Where lies the kingdom built for man,
    And where—oh, where's the Power.

BELIEVING IN EASTER

Oh, I believe in Easter
    With all my heart and soul.
Without its joyful message,
    My life would have no goal . . .

I'd roam, an aimless earthling,
    Just putting in my time,
Without the risen Savior
    To show the Way sublime.

What matters fame or fortune?
    What matters mere success
If Easter isn't pointing
    To what we each possess?

For hope to vanquish sorrow,
    For sin to fade from sight,
For love that lasts forever,
    Hold on to Easter—tight!

OBSERVING EASTER

It seems we've hardly caught our breath
    From thoughts of Christmas Day.
The spanning space from birth to death
    Is such a little way:
We start with shepherds in a cave—
    Our journey faith-ward bound—
And trust that we will share a grave
    Like that the Marys found.

58

WITHOUT EASTER?

If it hadn't been for Easter
    Would the star of Christmas glow?
If it hadn't been for Easter
    Would we ever rightly know
Of the shepherds and the wisemen
    And the manger near the inn—
Or the Lad who awed the temple—
    If that Easter hadn't been?

If it hadn't been for Easter
    Would His miracles remain—
Would the message of His teaching
    Be so permanent and plain?
Would we know He was our Savior;
    That He came to conquer sin
And to leave us with His promise—
    If that Easter hadn't been?

EMMAUS ROAD

Christ walked with two
    Who knew Him well
        Along that dusty path.
What He'd been through
    He heard them tell:
        His death and aftermath.

Confused, bereft,
    Bowed down with grief—
        Their eyes upon the soil,
What had they left
    But mixed belief
        In Him they thought was royal?

They argued some
    As they conversed
        Upon that Easter Day
'Bout Him who'd come
    And known man's worst,
        But failed to look His way.

Make me wide-eyed
    That I may know,
        Though heavy be my load,
He's at my side
    The while I go
        Down my Emmaus Road.

Luke 24: 13-17

IN ESSENCE

With even disposition,
    She does what she must do.
No envy or suspicion
    Beclouds her daily view.

She's patient and forgiving.
    She's tolerant and fair.
She adds more joy to living
    Because she seems to care.

She gladly answers duty
    Without a fault to find.
She looks for love and beauty
    And pays back good in
kind.

Life's best gets her attention—
    Her praise sincere and free.
She is—I pause to mention—
    The girl I'd like to be.

THE ETERNAL COMPROMISE

Two bikes went by that caught my eye.
    The first a mother rode.
With fiddle case she set the pace
    For him with diff'rent load.

A ball and mitt quite clearly fit
    Behind his mobile seat.
What pain and joy can snare a boy
    And for his youth compete!

THE ETERNAL ECHO

This morn we hear an echo
That travels hill to hill
Defying time and distance
By growing louder still.
Though earth has heard its message
Through years a hundred score,
We pause to catch that echo
And call it back once more.

This morn the belfry shouts it.
The wind picks up the strain
And with a voice once frosty
Seems warm with its refrain.
The choirs in full regalia
March up each church's aisle
To sing the selfsame echo
In much the same old style.

This morn the hearts inside us,
The small, the strong, the weak,
Are made a lot more happy
To hear that echo speak.
Let's keep its pledge unbroken.
Let's keep its creed unfurled,
And let us swell the echo—
"Merry Christmas to the world!"

THE ETERNAL MESSAGE

Once again in joy and wonder
　　We approach the holy tomb
Where despair's been rent asunder,
　　Where but glory lights the gloom,
Where the Marys went at dawning
　　On that week's initial day,
Where the sepulcher is yawning
　　For its stone's been rolled away.

Once again the angel motions
　　To the faithful to draw near
And to offer their devotions
　　For the news, "He is not here!
He has risen! Be not fearful.
　　As He promised He has done.
Be not sick at heart or tearful.
　　His great victory is won."

Once again we thank Our Master
　　For the message Easter gives.
Though there's heartbreak and disaster
　　For each one of us who lives,
We can glimpse eternal portals
　　Through a faith which makes it known
That what means the most to mortals
　　Isn't earth-bound by a stone.

FAITH

Unheard, unseen,
   I must believe
      What God sent Christ to tell.
It has to mean
   That I'll receive
      Reward for doing well—
For seeking out
   My Master's will,
      Converting it to mine,
And with no doubt
   Proceed to fill
      My cup from His divine.
My finite mind—
   Too weak to grasp
      The purpose of it all—
Shall stretch to find
   His rod to clasp.
      It must or I shall fall.

FACES OF FAITH

Many the faces of faith that look
Up to their God from a diff'rent book.
Many the knees that are bent to pray.
Each in their own, independent way.

Many the dialect, brogue, and tongue
Rise up to God on a lusty lung,
Singing His praises with humble heart,
Asking His blessing on paths they chart.

Many the temple, the church, the kirk
Covers the worshipers come to work
Deep in the vineyard of earthly good,
All seeing God as He meant they should.

May Our Dear Father so place His Hand
That it will keep and preserve this land
Where all the faces of faith may look
Up to their God from a diff'rent book.

FATHERS' PRAYER

"Dear Lord and Father of mankind
    Forgive our foolish ways."
Give us the sight that we combined
Shall have the will to go and find
    Thy Will this day of days.

Let every father 'mong us sip
    From faith forever true
And feel the strength that meets the lip—
The soul-felt sense of partnership
    In what he holds with You.

Today each looks with love and pride
    Upon his little clan.
Oh, let him know that glow inside—
That proof he is Your kind of guide—
    So precious to a man.

May those of us just starting out
    Remember homes we've had,
Resolving to make ours devout,
A tribute that will leave no doubt
    As to our kind of Dad.

Help us to build with fam'ly flame
    Our heritage of clay
So it will bear no future blame
But lead lives worthy of Your name.
    This is our prayer today.

THE FIFTH FREEDOM

The conveyance is fast
That can travel the past
   With no windows
      confining the view.
There's a scene 'long the way
That I conjure today.
   And it's one that all
      mothers pass through.

For to each there's a time
That is simply sublime.
   To anticipate makes
      mothers drool!
When it comes—blessed shock—
All emotions unlock:
   When the last one
      has gone off to school.

THE FIVE POINTS

May the justice of God
    Be the justice you give.
May His truth be your rod,
    Making truth what you live.
May His purity shine
    To illumine your soul.
May His love, love divine,
    Embrace you and your goal.
May His faith find its trade
    In your faith 'til it's plain
God must know you weren't made
    In His image in vain.

OUR FLAG

Her fifty stars send forth their light
    To dot her field of blue,
Much as the dawn drains off the night,
    They leave a lighter hue.
Her thirteen bars are like the rays
    A-welcoming the sun,
Recalling her historic days
    And glories she has won.

Yes, she's an early morning flag—
    This symbol of our worth—
A rising hope that must not sag
    But represent on earth
The very best free men can claim
    From their God-given lives—
The nation with the noblest name
    Whose noonday yet arrives.

Oh, she is young—this flag of ours.
    She's young in peopled youth.
She's young in scientific powers.
    She's young in finding truth.
God, keep her young to strongly grow
    Toward all the future holds,
But let a bit we oldsters know
    Too ripple in her folds!

FOLLOWING?

Do we follow where He leads us
    In the daily things we do?
Do we walk behind the Master
    In the precepts we pursue?
Are we kind in all our dealings—
    Kind enough for Him to see?
Are we gracious and forgiving
    As true Christian folks should be?

Do we follow—we, "the faithful"?
    Are we moving in His train?
Are we searching for His shadow
    Or our own self-centered gain?
Do we seek to find His footprints,
    Though it be a hilly climb,
Or complain that we're too weary
    Or we just don't have the time?

Do we follow or just linger
    In the thought of doing good?
If we'd really pause and ponder,
    We could follow, if we would.
But it takes both heart and hustle
    If we hope that we'll be found
By the Lord who bid us follow
    When He takes a look around.

THE FORMULA

Given a country
    once virgin of soil,
Veined underneath
    with rare metals and oil,
Laced well with rivers
    and lake-dotted scenes,
Splendid with mountains
    and valleys and streams.

Given a land
    to which pioneers came,
Lending their spirit
    and freedom of aim,
Willing to battle
    to save what is right,
Striving to keep
    all its precepts in sight.

Given a nation
    that's tried to be best,
One that the Lord
    has so bountif'lly blest—
What do ingredients
    like these portray?
What do you have
    but the U.S. of A.?

THE MAKING OF A FRIEND

Looking down on creation God heeded
   The anguish of those all alone,
And He felt that assistance was needed
   To supplement that of His own;
So He molded an ear for receiving
   Their problems, their wond'rings of "why".
Then He added for those who were grieving
   A shoulder on which they could cry.
Willing hands were equipped to be ready.
   A heart on which He could depend
Was implanted and warmed and made steady.
   That's how He created a friend.

FRIENDSHIP

Friendship is a handclasp
    Pressed to make it feel
Deep inside two beings
    There is something real
Sought to be translated—
    Carried through by touch—
That the hearts that send it
    Mean it very much.

Friendship is a letter
    Mailed across the miles
Bearing news from others
    Summoning their smiles,
Raising for the reader
    Thoughts worth thinking of,
For what lies unwritten
    Are the lines of love.

Friendship is a presence
    Seen or only felt
When a soul is laden
    With what will not melt
Or with what is happy
    And a joy to bear.
Friendship is the fusion
    Of folks who really care.

FRINGE BENEFITS

Fresh lilacs for the teacher!
    So fragrant their perfume—
These symbols of the season
    When earth begins to bloom.
Oh, teacher, breathe in deeply
    So this you will recall
Until you get an apple
    When you come back next fall.

GANDERING

It's not a bus, a car, a plane—
And thoughts to board it are in vain;
But high above on scheduled flight
The "Southward Special" comes in sight.
It sails across the trackless sky
With independent parts that fly
And honk along as if to say,
"Don't trespass on our right of way."
And when the shuttle's sound has died,
It seems that summer thumbed a ride.

75

GET THE PICTURE?

Here we are by the plane—
    On the boat—by the car.
Here we are in the rain
    Back a little too far.
Here we are with some folks
    Whom we'd only just met—
Full of fun—full of jokes,
    But their names we forget.

Here we are in a town—
    Can't think now what it's called.
Here the sun made us frown.
    Here's the bus that got stalled.
This one isn't too good.
    See those two little dots.
That's where both of us stood
    On historical spots.

Here we stayed over night,
    But it's 'round on the back . . .
Second room from the right
    By a trolley car track.
Here's a mountain snow-capped.
    We can't tell you just where;
But a trip that you've snapped
    Is a trip you can share.

GIFT OF SOUL

Within me, God, You've put a gift—
    An unseen sense of soul;
So You may enter in and lift
    All that which makes me whole.

This gift is more than mind and heart.
    Yet it controls them both.
A soul is special—set apart—
    Affecting inner growth.

You speak to it as to the seeds
    That burst at Your command.
Your spirit fills the mortal needs
    Of souls that understand.

Oh, God, I pray Your Spirit dwell
    Within my soul today,
Directing me toward doing well:
    Toward seeing things Your way.

      Ye are not in the flesh, but in
      the Spirit, if so be that the
      Spirit of God dwell in you.
      Now . . . the Spirit is life . . .

           —Romans 8:9-10

77

GIVE ME A REASON

I believe in the best.
    I believe in the good:
That, when put to the test,
    We will find brotherhood
Is the mixture of strength,
    The solution that glues
All our parts, and, at length,
    It's the one we will use.

I believe in the waving
    Of red, white and blue,
And in truly behaving
    As though it is due.
Of its hist'ry I'm proud.
    It's but us when we're pure.
May it never be bowed
    To the ones who aren't sure.

I believe that our God
    Answered pioneer prayers
When He unsealed our sod
    To improve man's affairs,
And, by favor of birth,
    I am free to achieve.
Is there reason on earth
    Why I shouldn't believe?

GOD'S FACE

God's great face shines through the seasons
    As they march around the year,
Dwarfing man and all his reasons
    Why such miracles appear.

It's reflected in each flower,
    In each egg a robin lays.
We can see it in the power
    Of the sun's life-giving rays.

God is watching peace and plunder
    From the stars that stud the night,
And His face is in the wonder
    Of the world of waking light.

God looks down on grief and sorrow
    With compassion in His eyes,
Knowing faith in His tomorrow
    Is the comfort of the wise.

Yes, God's face is always present
    And forever it's been thus.
Let us pray His view is pleasant
    When He's looking down at us.

GOLDEN MOMENT

The golden moment crowning life,
　　The brand on fifty years
Belonging to a man and wife,
　　Uncommonly appears.

It is a very special prize
　　Bestowed upon the few—
The years that mount until the eyes
　　Behold the golden view.

From this high peak two people see
　　The fields of former days—
The patchwork left by memory
　　Beneath the golden haze.

The best and worst, the joy and pain,
　　Are blended from this height.
The dark but makes the outline plain
　　Of what was sweet and bright.

It's but a moment briefly told,
　　A moment loved ones share,
A moment God has painted gold
　　To give a faithful pair.

GOLDEN YEAR

Dear God, since days forever old,
Your precious things You've painted gold.
The sun that differs nights from days
Gives light and life with golden rays.
Forsythia and daffodil
Are golden heralds of Your will.
Your harvest lesson is made plain
With golden ears and golden grain.
The maxim lent us as our tool
Is ever called the "Golden Rule".
When we cut centuries in twain
To mark accomplishment and gain,
We borrow from what seems Your test
To celebrate us at our best;
So, God, today draw very near
And bless for us our Golden Year.

Amen

THE GOOD FIGHT

I listened to him reminisce—
A bit of that—a bit of this,
   Remembered from his past:
His boyhood days—the hours of toil;
His study years—the "midnight oil",
   His youth by hardship cast.

I heard him as he talked aloud
Of what he'd built—what made him proud:
   Achievement out of strife.
I only wished that every youth
Could have this great rewarding truth
   To warm his later life.

The pride of having "what it takes"—
Not that of getting lucky breaks:
   The tackling what is hard,
The working for the "hopeless" goal
In time creates the rugged role
   That wins the world's regard.

"GOOD" FRIDAY

They buried Him, Our Jesus Christ,
    This day long years ago.
They buried Him so sacrificed—
    So hurt by word and blow,
So spat upon, so sorely mocked,
    So plied with whip and curse
That to this hour the world is shocked.
    No treatment could be worse.

They buried Him who'd trudged the street
    With cross upon His back,
Who'd suffered nails in hands and feet,
    Who'd felt the awful rack
As thorns pierced deeply in His head,
    As knife blade plunged His side,
As painfully He'd hung and bled
    Until at last He'd died.

They buried Him within a tomb
    And then they went away.
Oh, tell me, how could one presume
    Much "Good" in such a day?
But good there was in what was done—
    Outlasting human breath.
They didn't know, but with God's Son
    They also buried death.

GOOD OLD DAYS?

I remember the pump
    that we had to prime
And the day that a hamburger
    cost a dime.
I remember the streetcar
    that bounced the track
And the peddler who cried
    from his shabby hack
That his wares were fresh fish
    of the finest kind,
And the smell's even fresh
    in my mulling mind.

I remember the milk wagon's
    measured tread,
When its engine was sugar
    and apple fed;
When we kids had to walk
    if we would arrive
'Cause the mothers we drew
    hadn't learned to drive.
It was Sunday when all of us
    took a ride
In the car with its vases
    on either side.

I remember when dinner
    took time to fix
Because no one had thought
    of a ready-mix;
When an atom was something
    no man could split.
I remember lots more,
    but I must admit
I'm glad I remember
    all this—and how!
'Cause it makes me appreciate
    living now.

A GARDENER

One who works with living beauty,
    As created by our Lord,
Never feels the reins of duty
    Nor the doom of being bored;
For the soul is somehow seeded
    By the sight of buds and shoots
Til the spirit gets what's needed
    For the growth of human roots.

GOSPEL BY GEESE

A flapping, feathered arrowhead
    Flew shaftless 'cross the sky,
And pointed southward as it sped
    With plaintive, honking cry—
Propelled once more by faultless aim
    and power from a bow;
Like that which man can never claim
    And never truly know.

A GRANDMA APPLE TREE

An apple tree—well past her prime—
With limbs held low for tykes to climb
And sit upon her ample lap—
Has lost her mood to take a nap.
Instead she's holding in her arms
Two youngsters smitten by her
charms.
She winks to see them munch her fruit
And thinks their pilf'ring "kinda cute".

GRANDMA'S BOOK

My Grandma kept the Bible out
    Where everyone could see.
Her thoughts of it were so devout
    She felt that It should be
Where it would dominate the room,
    Reminding those who passed
Of virtues that they should assume
    And hold to very fast.

With rev'rent hand my Grandma took
    Her pen and deftly wrote
Upon the flyleaf of The Book
    All fam'ly days of note—
The birth and death and wedding date
    Of each within the clan,
The items big enough to rate
    The Book God gave to man.

My little Grandma, I recall,
    Would take an unsought nap
In sunset years and shoulder shawl
    With Bible in her lap.
Would hearts and minds be so instilled
    That faith and freedom shine
If this, our land, had not been filled
    With grandmas just like mine?

HE KNOWS

As we long "for the touch
   Of a vanished hand
And the sound of a voice that's still,"
May our thinking be such
   That we understand
Greater Wisdom and Perfect Will
Knows the depth of our grief,
   Knows that we are frail,
Knows how empty our heart's abyss,
Knows we cling to belief
   That He will not fail—
He who once gave the life we miss.

MY HEART IS YOURS

I give my heart unto your care,
Love cushioned so that it may bear
What time may ask a heart to share.

It's yours—this sign of what I bring—
Not as a blatant, boasting thing—
But silent as the budding spring.

It's yours—with all its youthful beat
Pulsating promises so sweet
That will perpetually repeat.

It's yours to add to joys that be.
It's yours because you've chosen me.
It's yours for all eternity.

HELP ME TO LISTEN

Lord, help me to listen to others who speak . . .
Others with voices both blatant and meek,
Others who tell me what I like to hear
Or, in the converse, what rankles my ear.

Lord, help me listen with seemly respect,
Listen intently for I may detect
Something important You're saying to me . . .
Using the speaker to amplify Thee.

HELP ME TO PRAY

Oh, please help me to pray.
    Let my weary soul kneel
At Your altar today,
    And allow me to feel
You are present, Oh, Lord—
    Very near to my side—
And will help me to ford
    Petty purpose and pride.

Make my pretense bow down.
    Bend the knees of my doubt.
Wipe the furrowing frown
    And the self-righteous pout
From the face that I wear
    As I turn it to You,
With the problems I bear
    And the fears that I view.

Help my spirit submit
    To Your breath—to Your word.
Let me listen to it
    Til my being is stirred
With the knowledge I need:
    With the will and the way
You would have me succeed.
    Oh, dear Lord, help me pray.

HERITAGE OF HOME

The first school, the first church,
    The first haven on earth
Is no object of search.
    It's the home of our birth.
It is there we first learn,
    As a bit of a tyke,
Through parental concern,
    What God's love must be like.

It is there we are fed
    Food for stomach and heart,
Where our first words are said
    And our first longings start,
Where no sham is employed,
    Where of pretense we're bared,
Where our joys are enjoyed
    And our sorrows are shared.

Be it rich—be it poor
    Matters little to youth
If within there's a store
    Of pure warmth, trust and truth.
And the cycle's complete
    When the youngsters are grown
If all this they repeat
    In the homes of their own.

HI! MOMMA!

Some days are rather strenuous
    All mothers will agree.
To little problems that we face
    There is no master key.
My youngster used to stop me short
    When caught at something bad.
He'd greet me in his sweetest tone
    Before I could get mad,
        "Hi! Momma!"

I'd think I heard a cupboard door
    And venture in to look
Just as that roguish little elf
    To heels a-flying took.
A gumdrop on the table lay.
    He'd dropped it in his flight.
Far out of range he'd call back words
    That would deny his plight,
        "Hi! Momma!"

'Twould be a quiet afternoon
    At nap time's very peak
When suddenly a toy he loved
    Began to roll and squeak.
Around the corner Mother came
    To see who was about.
There was a scrambling back to bed
    And guiltless little shout,
        "Hi! Momma!"

I pondered on his errant ways
    With psychologic thought.
He couldn't get those traits from me
    Or things that he'd been taught.
Just as I tried along these lines
    Upon some clue to seize,
His Daddy wandered in from work,
    And his first words were these,
        "Hi! Momma!"

HIS FAITH AND MINE

Can I, a creature God has made,
    Deny my trust in Him?
Can I by doubt be so betrayed—
    Can reason grow so dim—
Can love so lose its lucent link—
    Can I so faithless be
When I am sure, if I but think,
    My God has faith in me.

He's put me on His rolling sphere
    With all its native wealth,
Surrounded me with folks held dear,
    Provided me with health,
Bestowed what talents I possess,
    Sent hope in full degree;
So, truthfully, I must confess
    My God has faith in me.

But faith is something that implies
    The sort of binding trust
On which another soul relies
    Because it's good and just.
My faith in God shall never swerve,
    Though oft I cannot see
What I should do so I'll deserve
    The faith He has in me.

HIS FIRST REGARD

The wrong was done.
The rising sun
    Erased all thoughts of gloom
Because it shone
Upon a stone
    Before an empty tomb.

But where was He
Of Galilee,
    Our Lord no longer dead?
He wasn't there,
But tell me where
    Had He, our Savior sped?

He didn't go
To find His foe
    And even up the score.
He didn't seek
The wicked weak
    And curses on them pour.

To those who cried
Because He died,
    The folks who called Him "friend",
With them He chose
When He arose
    His glory hour to spend.

Though scorned and scarred,
His first regard
    Was not revenge or grief,
But making glad
The sorely sad
    With proof that sealed belief.

HIS KNOWLEDGE

Palm Sunday gave Him long and loud
The plaudits of a fickle crowd.
    It hailed Him as a king.
He humbly rode a humble mount
Past multitudes too large to count
    He knew would turn and sting.

He knew His love would soon be tried,
Betrayed, deserted and denied
    By those who shared that day.
He knew the palms before Him spread
Would turn to thorns to pierce His head.
    He knew His future way.

He knew what He would have to face
At hands of mortals cruel and base.
    He knew it very well.
And yet He rode with stoic calm
Along that path of quilted palm
    And heard His praises swell.

How awful must such knowledge be!
How horrible if such as we
    Were told our future load.
We see our burden bit by bit,
But God showed Jesus all of it.
    No palm could hide His road.

HOLY TIME

A wedding, Lord, is holy time:
    The blending of two souls
Who ask Your blessing sweet, sublime,
    Upon their merging roles.

A little child's baptismal day
    Is holy time. It's true
Because we hope small lives will stay
    With child-like love of You.

A time of death—a time of grief—
    Is holy time. Yes, Lord,
Deep holy time that tests belief
    And trusts in Your reward.

In church each holy day we share
    Is holy time aloud,
Proclaimed in sermon, song and prayer—
    The worship of a crowd.

But, Lord, beyond what's met by most
    Are hills for each to climb.
Hear single voices in the host,
    And grant them holy time.

HOLY WEEK

The very worst that man could do
    He did unto his Father's Son.
As Holy Week comes into view,
    We mark with meaning what was done.

The Sunday palms and flatt'ring cheers
    Before that woeful week could die
Were mock'ry's echoes, jibes and jeers,
    And cursing cries of "Crucify!"

With arms outstretched upon the cross,
    He seemed to reach around the earth
With love not lessened by His loss,
    But destined to embrace its girth.

His blood shed there upon the hill—
    Blood spurting for a soldier's knife—
Throughout the world is flowing still,
    As it transfuses Christian life.

This Holy Week—this awful week—
    Repeats for all who pause and pray
The truth that, if in faith they seek,
    They, too, will have their Easter Day.

A HOME

Where two will toil together
    To make their human nest
Withstand life's windy weather
    And be a place of rest . . .

A center of affection
    Where children love and learn
And find in restrospection
    The truths to which they turn . . .

A bond of interweaving
    The all that touches each;
A trust, a true believing
    In everybody's reach . . .

A spell that's cast forever
    Upon the ones who roam,
For time and space can't sever
    The mem'ry of a home.

HOPE

Hope is the dawn of tomorrow
    Bringing unblemished a day,
Stained by no streaking of sorrow,
    Dulled by no dents of dismay.

Hope is the light of all living,
    Never admitting the dark,
Downing despair and misgiving,
    Calling, "Come, look, there's a spark".

Hope is the youth of a nation.
    Hope is the spring of the year.
Both from their seeds of creation
    Grow without feeling of fear.

Hope is the drive in our dreaming.
    Hope is the lure to achieve.
Hope is the ransom redeeming
    Problems that injure and grieve.

Hope is the faith of a mortal
    Letting him lean on its rod,
Propping him portal to portal
    Up to the promise of God.

A HOUSEWIFE'S PRAYER

Dear Lord Who once brought forth the food
To feed a hungry multitude,
Forgive the grumbling you survey
When I prepare three meals a day.

Oh, You Who cleansed from man his sin,
Give strength to me as I begin
To wash the dishes, clothes and floors
And do my countless household chores.

Oh, You Who asked the children near,
Bless those I love and hold most dear.
Put patience in my teaching too
Until in thought they come to You.

Oh, You Who suffered untold pain,
Be merciful when I complain
About some little hurt I have.
Make love and faith its healing salve.

Oh, You Who gave Your life to good,
Help me to help my neighborhood,
My church, my friends, and those who need.
Help me and mine to live Your creed.

Oh, Lord Who left Your heav'nly home
Because Our Father bid You roam,
Make this, our dwelling, truly blest
By living with us as our guest.

HURRY UP BOY

I am fond of a lad
Still untutored by school
Who, when called by his dad,
Lags a bit—as a rule.
Being urged to more speed,
(With no thought to be coy)
He was heard to concede,
"I'm a hurry up boy!"

"Hurry up" has become
Like a part of his name.
Though it bothers him some,
He's relaxed just the same,
Still unknowing that strife
Will with time quench this joy
And will cast him for life
As a "hurry up boy".

HUSBANDRY

He's worried 'bout the weather now.
    Do rain clouds seem in sight?
Does one suppose that he should plow
    Or irrigate tonight?
It's quite a chore for him to keep
    A two by eight expanse
Containing what he hopes to reap
    From three tomato plants.

They're blushing some the while they grow,
    Embarrassed as can be,
Because he brags about them so
    And bids the neighbors see
What agriculture could achieve
    By following his stance.
Just look, if you should disbelieve,
    At three tomato plants.

No worm would dare invade his crop.
    He'd meet it eye to eye
With such a glare that it would stop
    Its burrowing to cry.
He's even reading farm reports
    And probing federal grants.
There must be subsidies of sorts
    For three tomato plants.

INTERPRETIVE ART

The world of art has mysterious ways
        When it pauses to judge its peers;
But I propose for a word of praise
        A design worth a round of cheers:
Two snowball eyes and a snowball nose
        And a mouth that is curved in glee
Were mitten-patted until they froze
        On the bark of an old oak tree.

I looked and laughed, and it laughed right back,
        As we stood peering face to face.
Whatever talent this work might lack,
        In my book it deserves first place.
I'm sure the artist had no deep goal.
        It was meant as a snow-time joke;
But let me think that his secret soul
        Caught a dream of the sleeping oak!

INVOCATION

Dear Lord,
For the promise of the sunrise,
    For the power in a seed,
For the fragrance of a flower,
    And the challenge of a weed,
For the songs You wrap in feathers
    And send forth on colored wings,
Lord, we are so grateful
    That the center of us sings.

For the hope that keeps us trying,
    For the loyalty of friends,
For the purpose that we gather
    And the benefit it lends,
We're indebted for Your blessing—
    For the sanction of Your touch—
And we join our hearts to tell You
    That we thank You—very much!

JANUARY

Young Janny is a blust'ry kid
 With muffler 'neath his nose.
The rascal in him isn't hid
 As well as he'd suppose.
He frosts the windows, stalls the cars,
 Blows folks like us about,
And with all comers gladly spars
 And gives the vict'ry shout.

The Mom of Months just shakes her head.
 He's hers with whom to cope.
She watches him arrive with dread,
 But still she knows there's hope.
He's immature like any youth,
 Untried but free from fear . . .
A little rough, but still, in truth,
 A challenge to the year.

JULY

July is a soldier saluting his flag;
So proud of his country he's given to brag
'Bout all of her virtues, her wisdom, her lore:
A swain to the lady he's come to adore.

July can relax in his own summer sun,
Completely ignoring what ought to be done.
He relishes picnics and ballgames and such.
Vacations and gard'ning he likes very much.

July, as a person, is youth at high time,
Developing fully but not at his prime.
He's vibrant, warm-hearted, and eager to try.
Life's harvest is still but a gleam in his eye.

THE KISSING TIME

At the end of the day for our troupe of two,
    When they're ready to go to sleep,
There's a ritual set that we all go through—
    One we'd love to forever keep.
It is then that our leg-weary lass and lad
    Who've been parted from daily grime
Will arrive on the scene—all pajama clad—
    To partake in the kissing time.

Both ascend Daddy's lap in a single bound.
    Each has lips in a pleated bud
That is aimed to connect with a smacking sound
    And deposit a juicy flood.
If their Grandma or Grandpa should be on hand,
    There's the joy of more laps to climb,
For the fam'ly's theirs and receives their brand
    At the "round-up" of kissing time.

When they've taken a kiss and have passed one out
    Like two bees on a pollen beat,
Is there any around who would have a doubt
    That the honey of love is sweet?
Is there any on earth who would choose to miss
    How the bells in the heart can chime
When they're started to swing by a baby kiss
    At the stroke of the kissing time?

LADIES TO LUNCH

If you think that some sort of
    an ailment
    Has just suddenly struck at
      your spouse;
If her efforts permit no curtailment
    When it comes to her grooming
      the house;
If she passes you by in a hurry
    As though something had dealt
      her a punch,
Let me say there's no reason
    to worry.
      She's but having the ladies
      to lunch.

If the silver is out of seclusion,
    And it's rubbed to a shimmering
      shine;
If the kitchen is fraught with
      confusion,
    And there's no place to pause
      or recline;
If you feel you've been turned out
    of clover
      While she cries 'cause the
      crunchies won't crunch;
These are hurdles you'll have to
    get over
      For she's having the ladies
      to lunch.

(Continued on next page)

If routine has been set all asunder,
But the fragrance of food is
a treat
'Til the wife of your life starts to
wonder
If you'll go to a restaurant
to eat;
If you haven't determined the
matter,
You'll be right if you cherish
the hunch
That for dinner you'll find on
your platter
What the ladies bequeath you
from lunch.

"LAW—BRIDGE TO JUSTICE"

There's a bridge across the ages,
    O'er the vast ravine of time,
Built with effort born of sages
    To a structure most sublime.

Like a rainbow 'bove the river
    Of dissension and distrust,
It gives promise to deliver
    Those who cross it what is just.

It's an arch with sturdy pilings
    Pounded firmly in the past
That's withstood the sharp revilings
    Of a frequent stormy blast.

There are those who'd swim around it
    So's to sooner reach the shore,
But in floundering have found it
    As a frame they can't ignore.

Future traffic will be heavy
    As life's loads and men increase.
On its strength will be the levy
    Of a traveler called Peace.

There are planks that need replacing,
    And a few could stand a nail.
Here and there a little bracing
    Might be used to good avail.

We who love it should be banded
    To protect the bridge from loss
Or someday we'll find we're stranded
    With no way to get across.

FOR OUR LEADERS

Dear God, please hear us as we pray
For those who lead us day by day,
    For those around the earth
On whom the people—every shade
In all the nations You have made—
    Depend for lives of worth.

No leader has an easy task,
And that is why, Oh, God, we ask
    Your help in what is done.
May those with Christian precepts feel
That Your support is very real
    And seek it through Your Son.

And through our prayers may leaders who
Have never shared our view of You
    Be moved to work for good
Til all the peoples everywhere
Can reap the purpose of this prayer:
    A peaceful brotherhood.

LEFT OVERS

I was thinking tonight
    After dishes were done
How my belt was so tight
    And to breathe wasn't fun.
Now my meal was discreet—
    Even small in amount;
But the leavings I eat
    I'm afraid are what count.

I've my conscience to blame
    That I'm growing so stout
'Cause it seems such a shame
    To throw anything out.
When the rest haven't room
    For their rolls or their cake,
It is I who consume
    What the garbage should take.

When I add for the day
    What I glean from my mate
Who with will lets it stay
    On the side of his plate,
Plus my son's bit of pie
    And my daughter's French toast,
It's no wonder that I
    Am becoming "the most".

LENTEN PRAYER

Dear God,

Behind the Savior whom You sent
    Your faithful trace the way
Illumined by the lamp of Lent
    That shines 'til Easter day.
We seek each vestige left by him
    Who first explained the role
Of that which never deigns to dim—
    A man's immortal soul.

Oh, help us walk the well-worn path
    Through triumph, hate, and death
Unto the wondrous aftermath
    When, with eternal breath,
He spoke to those who followed then,
    Revealing his great goal:
The brotherhood of mortal man,
    Each conscious of a soul.

Oh, let the light of Lent attract
    The souls of all who love—
The souls of all who see in fact
    Their source in You above.
In them revive, replant, renew,
    Much as You do the sod,
With springtime strength and faith to do.
    This is our prayer, Oh, God.

LET IT GROW

If your plan is just beginning,
Don't abandon hope of winning
   'Cause it's slow.
Like a bud first feeling power,
It needs time to be a flower.
   Let it grow!

At the source of every river
Is a little trickling sliver
   Of a flow.
Miles away with force it rages
Because Nature through the ages
   Let it grow.

For an egg the trust is clinging
It will yield a creature winging
   High and low;
Yet a bird sits on it queenly
With an instinct to serenely
   Let it grow.

Every baby is destructive
Long before he is productive,
   As you know;
So don't drop your hope of winning
If your plan is just beginning,
   Let it grow.

A LETTER TO LINCOLN

February 12th

Dear Mr. Lincoln,

So much of prose—so much of verse
    Has been in praise of you
That it's become a writer's curse
    To find a thought that's new.
No other life has been so probed
    And analyzed by men.
No other life has been so robed
    In glory by the pen.

Your rise from such a meager start,
    Your honesty and wit,
The humbleness of your great heart,
    Your will to never quit,
Your leadership that once preserved
    This nation as a whole,
Your love of man that never swerved
    From its near sacred goal—

All this you've heard us yearly tell
    Upon your day of birth.
By now your heart must truly swell
    Or else be filled with mirth
A-list'ning to the candidates
    As each makes his debut
Expounding in what he orates
    How he compares to you.

LET'S THANK HIM

"The Lord hath done great things for us"
    Whereof we're glad today.
For harvest rich and bounteous,
    Let's thank Him as we pray.

Let's thank Him for the ripened fruit,
    The gathered golden grain,
The seasons marching resolute
    To make His promise plain.

Let's thank Him for all earthly wealth,
    For friends and fam'ly love,
For happy homes and hope and health
    And faith in Him above.

Let's thank Him for that Pilgrim band
    Who braved an angry sea
To give the world its "promised land,"
    Its nation of the free.

"The Lord hath done great things for
us."
    Oh, let them be reviewed,
And let each heart be copious
    With love and gratitude.

LET US GIVE—

Oh, Lord, let us give
    What we have in our store
To others who live
    And are needing it more.
We've wealth we can spare
    Though it may not be gold.
We've treasure to share
    That we selfishly hold.

Oh, Lord, in man's grief,
    Let us give words of hope.
Our pledge of belief
    May help others who grope.
A sign that we trust
    What a dreamer would do
Is often the "must"
    That makes dreaming come true.

Oh, Lord, we have cheer;
    We have love; we have thought
To give those who fear.
    These can never be bought.
They're ours while we live.
    With Your promise in store:
As long as we give,
    You'll keep giving us more.

LIFE'S PURPOSE

Life must have a fuller meaning
    Than a self-preparing state—
Fuller far than just a weaning
    Into Heaven's Golden Gate,
For if that comprised its mission,
    We'd be happy marking time
Til the day of our transition
    To the shore of the sublime.

But instead we have a yearning
    To improve the human lot,
To apply ourselves to learning
    What is good and what is not
For the folks who live around us—
    Those who err and those who ail,
Those to whom Our Father's bound us
    With a faith that will not fail.

To each life He gave example
    Of how living should be done
When He sent the perfect sample
    In the person of His Son.
Not for self did Christ heal blindness,
    Not for self His words of worth,
But He tried through love and kindness
    To bring Heaven nearer earth.

THE LINCOLN MEMORIAL

Over the shoulder of Lincoln God stood
    All of the days of his life,
Whispering only of courage and good,
    Strengthening him for his strife.

Over his shoulder in marble He stands,
    Watching the great and the small
Coming from this and the world's other lands.
    Here they are equally tall.

Over his shoulder one hears Him to speak,
    "Here is my symbol of worth.
Here is the right and the might of the meek.
    Here is the best of the earth."

Those who look up feel a warmth in the stone,
    Feel a presence that's awesomely odd.
Lincoln, the statue, and they aren't alone.
    Over his shoulder is God.

LITTLE CROCUS

Little Crocus, poking through,
Would I were as brave as you.
You're the scout the tulips send
To report the winter's end.
Hyacinth and Daffodil
Fear the earth above is chill.
Underground the bulblets cheer
When they hear you volunteer,
You, who seem to have no fear.

Breaking ground with grass-like leaves,
You the snowy earth receives,
Smiling at your fragile form,
Smiling 'til itself is warm . . .
Warm enough to open up
Your wee funnel-fashioned cup.
"All is well", you notify
Those for whom you are the spy.
Then they, too, push toward the sky.

Little Crocus, I can see
Size of courage isn't wee
Just because a plant is small.
You're the bravest of them all.
They in all the hues God made
Soon will venture on parade,
But I wonder what they'd do
Without you to lead them through.
Would I were as brave as you!

LITTLE MISS MOMMA

She appeared at the door
    'Neath my Sunday chapeau,
And the slippers she wore
    Were a pair I should know.
The large purse in her hand
    Was my object of pride.
As she struggled to stand,
    With excitement she cried,
    "I'm Miss Momma".

Should possessions be saved
    At so costly a price
As to say she behaved
    In a manner not nice?
For what compliment paid
    Could have been more sincere
Than the one that she made,
    And I always shall hear:
    "I'm Miss Momma".

LITTLE YOU KNOW

Little you know as you
    walk down the street
All of the cares of the
    people you meet.
Hollow the joy that the
    features may show.
Hidden 'neath laughter
    lies many a woe.
Little you know!

Fear, pain and conflict—
    companions of life—
Fall into step on our
    highway of strife,
Shadow us ever in all
    that we do.
Should you believe
    they select only you,
Little you know!

Little you know—
    but in that lies the start.
Look at your fellows
    with that in your heart.
Then for their faults
    you'll more freely allow.
Where this might lead,
    if you started right now,
Little you know!

A LIVING FAITH

Make mine, Oh, Lord, a faith that lives—
    A faith that breathes with zeal—
A faith that functions, one that gives
    With usefullness that's real;
A faith that feels for fellow souls,
    That hears the call of need
In mundane or more lofty roles—
    Then answers it with deed.

Make mine a faith that lives and grows
    And speaks for honest good;
That truly sees where beauty shows
    In city, farm and wood.
Oh, make my faith the while I strive
    A faith that's poised to do—
One vital, vibrant and alive—
    Alive, Oh, Lord, as You.

James 2:26—"For as the body apart
        from the spirit is dead, so
        faith apart from works is
        dead."

LOOKING UP

Looking up—pushing out—
    Reaching forth with new growth—
Is what life's all about;
    Though at times we are loath
To admit or believe
    That we're just like the plants.
Looking up, we receive
    All the blessings God grants.

Come, Look up at the sun!
    If you're looking through tears,
That's how rainbows are won,
    That's how faith conquers fears.
Looking up day and night
    May not win you a crown,
But to face friendly light
    Surely beats looking down.

"LOUDER THAN WORDS"

My neighbor's planting tulips.
    She's down upon her knees
A-digging holes to hold them
    Before the sod can freeze.
Her pose—not meant as holy—
    Approaches it in fact.
Her faith—without her thinking—
    Is proven by her act.

LOVE

Love is a nod from across the room.
Love is a knowing wink.
Love is a laugh from the heart's full bloom.
Love is a pause to think
Selflessly, wholly, of what it shares.
Threaded by man and wife,
Quietly weaving 'til unawares
Love is the whole of life.

Love is an arm to support an arm.
Love wipes away a tear.
Love speaks of love with a special charm.
Love is a list'ning ear.
Love is the squeeze of a gentle hand,
Saying what words can't say.
Knowing such love makes one understand
God in a wiser way.

1 John 4:8—God is Love

THE MAN WHO LOVES A TREE

There's always something fine about
    A man who loves a tree.
The more I think the less I doubt
    They share a common key—
A key unlocking all the best
    That comes from earth and air,
A wholesomeness that's not expressed
    Of which they're both aware.

The man, so like the growing wood,
    Is rugged, strong and straight.
His thoughts are rooted well in good,
    His head too high for hate.
To brag or gloat he'd not pretend.
    He feels that he was made
To do his bit just like his friend
    That lends the world its shade.

Both man and tree expand and grow
    By braving sun and storm.
When winters come, both face the snow
    With faith that keeps them warm,
The faith that spring will soon begin,
    The faith that's full and free,
The faith that seems much stronger in
    The man who loves a tree.

MASTERS TO OWN

If I am owned by what I own,
    By what I'd hate to lose,
By what can hold me brain and bone,
    What masters would I choose?
I wouldn't want to be a slave
    To some but fleeting whim,
To something only fools would crave,
    Or living would be grim.

Some things I own were gifts to me—
    Like those of fam'ly ties.
Of course, I own them, yet you see,
    They're masters that I prize.
Beyond these gifts I have a choice,
    A freedom more or less,
To tell the world in clear-cut voice
    Just what I would possess.

I want a faith that nought transcends.
    I want a worthwhile goal.
I want a few good, honest friends
    To keep my spirit whole.
I want good books when I'm alone
    And beauty growing free.
All these I'd surely like to own;
    So they could master me.

MERRY CHRISTMAS

The sparkle from a pair of eyes
Lit up by Santa's sweet surprise,
A hearty laugh from one himself
Who acts a bit like that old elf,
A healthy home with spicy smells
That blend with pine, a few church bells,
Some cards, a visit from a friend,
A moment that you'll have to spend
Rereading Luke, some carols sung:
All this and more you'll find among
The wishes that I wish your way
To merry-up your Christmas Day.

MICHIGAN

"Look about you," says the motto
    Of the finest of the states,
A peninsula most pleasant
    With a wealth of wonder waits,
With a hist'ry like no other,
    Having flown four nations' flags.
If you look, you'll have no question
    Why a native sort of brags.

"Look about you" for a farmland
    That's as fertile as can be,
Where the beets and beans and cherries
    Bring a very handsome fee.
See the factories and forests.
    See the coal and copper mines.
See them peopled for the progress
    That their industry designs.

"Look about you!" See the beauty
    Of eleven thousand lakes.
See the shrines of higher learning
    And the paths a tourist takes.
If you seek a state of grandeur
    That the Lord has multi-blessed,
"Look about you" with assurance
    That you see the very best.

MORNING REVERIE

May the Lord look down
And not cast a frown
   On the things that
     I do today.
May I feel an hour
When I know His power
   Is behind what I
     think and say.

May my best shine through
In what I pursue.
   May my pettiness
     step aside.
Having done my best,
Should my goal be blest,
   Let me not be the
     pawn of pride.

Should the clouds close in
On what I begin
   Or the floods cover
     fields well sown,
May my spirit rise,
Well assured the skies
   Will be clear and
     His purpose known.

A MOTHER

With her being starts creation
　　Of a little mind and soul,
As she takes the obligation
　　Of her new expanding role.

From then on she walks with worry,
　　Some defeat and some success;
Oft with patience, oft with hurry,
　　All her lifetime, more or less.

When the object of her mission
　　Grows too big to hold her hand,
She still asks in sweet petition
　　God to lead and understand.

For to her there is no finish
　　To the job life bids her start.
Love by years does not diminish
　　Or outgrow a mother's heart.

MOTHERHOOD'S PRAYER

Oh, Lord, the kind of world to come
Must rest with him who sucks his thumb
    And hugs his teddy bear.
I know how much depends on me
To help him so that he will see
    What's pure and true and fair.

He watches every move I make.
He reaches up in trust to take
    My hand to be his guide.
Unquestioning, my words he hears.
To him I am the seer of seers.
    We're now each other's pride.

Too soon the playpen grows too small.
Then schools and occupations call,
    According to Your plan.
The time allotted me is short
In which to You I must report
    I'm giving You a man.

I love him more than I can tell.
Oh, Lord, help me to teach him well.
    I know my child is good.
And I shall always feel the blame
Should he not glorify Your name
    Because I'm Motherhood.

A MOTHER'S MEMORY

That squeezed and stemless first bouquet
Outshines the florist's prize today.
The pangs of mem'ry fairly shout
Of teeth that came and then came out,
Of school days, scouts, and baseball games,
Recitals, plays—and many names
Beclouded recollection skims
For adding little hers and hims—
Companions of the yesteryear
To those whose childhood I hold dear.

The holidays the while they grew,
The birthday celebrations too,
Their strengths, their quirks, their little flaws,
Their fears and hurts that gave me pause . . .
And then those graduation days
When they attained their grown-up phase!
But never will their lives outride
Their mother's worry or her pride.
Young mothers, heed the bad . . . the bliss:
Your time will come to reminisce.

MOTHERS

Dear God, please bless the Mom today
    Who holds upon her knee
The child who'll lead all folks to pray—
    The minister-to-be.

Bless her who's bandaging the thumb
    Of him whose tears are thick—
Of him who in the days to come
    Will heal his fellow sick.

Bless her who carries him about
    While shopping shelf by shelf.
Someday the squirming little sprout
    Will own a store himself.

Bless her who hears her own recite
    His homework or his speech,
Who knows that he must get it right
    Because someday he'll teach.

Bless her whose interest proves for him
    The catalyst he needs
To follow forth with all his vim
    Great scientific leads.

Bless her who cheers when he's at bat—
    The sandlot's pride and joy—
'Cause time will make him more than that.
    He'll be a big league's boy.

God, bless their efforts day by day.
    Assist in all they do
For this old world in every way
    Depends on them and You.

MOTHERS ALL

I was roused by a sound
    That came out of a tree.
'Twas a mother who spoke
    And she didn't agree
With some act of her son—
    Just a babe of a bird—
I so wished I might know
    Of the trouble I heard.

It was easy to see
    That her patience was spent,
But on what sort of woe
    Had her fledgling been bent?
Was he ripping the grass
    From the sides of the nest?
Was a feather now gone
    From the front of his breast?

Had she feared he was lost
    'Cause he'd vanished from sight?
Were his claws full of mud
    So he looked like a fright?
Did he turn up his beak
    At the worm she'd prepared?
Was his playing so rough
    That his sister was scared?

Could it be that a nap
    Was the cause of it all?
That he didn't come home
    When she started to call?
Well, whatever it was,
    I would like to report
In her moment of trial,
    She had gained my support!

"MY FATHER'S HOUSE"

May the Lord of Love
From His realm above
   Touch the hurt
      in your heart today.
May your faith look up
Like a holy cup
   To be filled
      in His wondrous way.

It is you who's lost
Not the one who's crossed
   The horizon
      of human hope
To the blessed shore
Of Forevermore.
   It is you
      who is left to grope.

In your hour of grief
Hold a firm belief
   In the promise
      Christ came to give.
There's no greater vow
To remember now
   And for all of
      the days you live.

A NATIONAL PRAYER

Oh, God, be good to this, our land,
    As You have always been.
Oh, help our leaders understand
    The worth that's meant to win.
Oh, let us know what You expect
    Each one of us to do.
Then lend the will and intellect
    For us to see it through.

Oh, God, we've been Your favored soil.
    Selected's been the seed
Of people born or sent to toil
    For this great country's need.
It's been the haven and the fort
    For all who would be free.
Oh, God, continue Your support.
    Protect its liberty.

We pray, as we have prayed before,
    For life that's blessed with peace,
For guidance from the ways of war,
    For bitterness to cease.
Be good to this small part of earth.
    Your benediction place
Upon the ones who'd make it worth
    The sanction of Your Grace.

OUR NATION'S HOMES

By its homes one knows a nation,
    Not its wisdom or its wealth,
And their strength in true relation
    Shows the nature of its health.
'Round the hearthstone, almost holy,
    Met the families of yore,
As they worshipped God who solely
    Guided ever hope and chore.

In its homes this land was nourished
    By the Bible and by bread
Til its minds and souls both flourished
    And its hearts were duly fed.
There regard was born for neighbors.
    There respect for elders dwelt.
There was respite from one's labors.
    There concern for each was felt.

From its homes came wholesome thinking
    That has made this country great
Down the generations linking
    To each other by this trait.
May our homes accept their duty
    In the future as the past,
Giving strength and inner beauty
    That allow a land to last.

NONE BUT THE FAITHFUL

Whom did they try all through the night,
Fearful that He would gain their might?
Who was the Man so meek and mild
Rulers and priests with hate reviled?
Slandered by words and scourged by whips,
Yet nought of malice left His lips,
Could He be more than mortal Jew?
None but the faithful really knew.

What of the tales that followed Him—
Strength for the halt and weak of limb,
Sight for the blind and lepers' cure,
Cleansing the sin from souls impure,
Raising the dead and giving hope?
Strange were the powers in His scope!
Could they be tricks magicians do?
None but the faithful really knew.

Who was the Man they crucified,
Centered with thieves on either side,
Crowned with a wreath that pricked His head,
Slashed so His side was flowing red,
Knowing the pangs of parching thirst,
Hearing the good He'd done now cursed?
Was it God's Son Who suffered so?
None but the faithful really know.

NUDGE ME!

What can I do, dear Lord, today
To ease another's troubled way?
    I hope You'll let me know.
The problem is I may not see
Just what to do or where to be.
    I pray 'twill not be so.

What's worse . . . I pray I shall not shun
A good that plainly should be done
    Because I fail to care . . .
Or that I turn my eyes aside
And act because of foolish pride
    As though it were not there.

It isn't easy to behave
With virtues lofty, sweet and brave.
    In fact, few mortals do.
Yet most of us aren't bad at heart—
Just need a push, a little start,
    A nudging, Lord, from You.

OCTOBER 31st

When we come to the end of October
    And the gold has been spent in the leaves,
There's a sense in the air sadly sober
    As though all of the atmosphere grieves.

In this pause there's a sort of suspension—
    A sensation of hanging between—
Til earth yawns so's to soften the tension,
    And emits a most mystical scene.

Little witches and goblins come screeching,
    As they cast on the neighbors a spell—
With their bags and their breathless beseeching,
    With the threat that we've come to know well.

In an hour or two it is ended.
    Earth inhales with sigh drowsy deep,
And October's no longer suspended.
    Like the children, it's full and asleep.

OLD BEAU

Our Bob once had a toy named "Beau."
    It was so soft and clean
When it was new, but very soon
    Its better days were seen.
He'd plucked off most the yellow fuzz.
    Its face got out of shape,
But still Bob ran to get it
    If he was in a scrape.

Yes, Beau was rather battered,
    And its covering was black
Where little hands had patted well,
    Sometimes with quite a whack.
To Bob, of course, there was no change.
    He saw no flaws appear.
The marks of weather, wear and time
    Just made Old Beau more dear.

At times I guess we feel that way
    About some friends we know
Who may not look like movie stars
    Or live on Wealthy Row;
And we don't care if they are old
    And not the least renowned
Because we feel much more secure
    When we have them around.

AN OLD TREE STUMP

Protruding from a nearby lawn
Two feet of stump beholds the dawn,
The day, the twilight and the dark:
A solid scar, unsightly stark.

Bereft of limbs and leafy crown
It can't reveal what brought it down.
Perhaps disease had spoiled its life,
Or it succumbed to stormy strife.

No longer can it do its best:
Give shade or hold a little nest,
Or share in every season's scene
Its beauty branched in gold or green.

Yet, as I pass it day by day,
It serves to make me pause and pray,
"Dear Lord of worth in man and tree,
Let nothing make a stump of me!"

ONCE MORE

Once more we hear the angels
    And hurry from the hills.
Once more the Star is shining
    And wisdom through us thrills.
Once more we've come to Christmas.
    The spirit of it glows
And fills us each with gladness
    No other season knows.

Once more we find the manger
    And kneel within our souls
To ask the Infant's blessing
    Upon our earthly roles.
Once more our love we offer
    To Him asleep on hay,
And find as we are leaving
    We take more love away.

FOR OPTIMISM

Oh, Lord, release me from this jail
    Where I've imprisoned me
By letting dismal thoughts prevail
    And granting them the key.

I've made my day a narrow cell
    By narrowing my mind
So my reflections only dwell
    On fault that I can find.

My energy is used in vain
    By knocking on the past.
Old hurts dissolve my strength in pain.
    My bars still hold me fast.

Renew in me the faith I need.
    Let hope become restocked
Until I know that I'll succeed
    And find my door unlocked.

PALM SUNDAY CROWD

We meet today
Upon the way
    To old Jerusalem.
We join in song
The gathered throng
    'Round Him of Bethlehem.
We stand beside
God's gentle guide
    Who rides a lowly ass.
We're 'mong the crowd
That cries aloud
    As He is due to pass.

Around us stand
The poor and grand,
    The brave and those with fears,
The sick and blind
And all inclined
    Throughout two thousand years
To come this far,
Where now we are,
    On soul and heart that fly,
And leave their load
Beside the road
    While He is riding by.

In manner calm
We spread the palm
    With lips that part in prayer.
We, too, propose
To spread our clothes
    Like all the others there.
Oh, Lord, we pray
Preserve this day.
    Let nought our minds becloud;
So that we seek
Within a week
    To join another crowd.

PATCH OF BLUE

Though breezes sigh and heavens cry
    And daylight dark descends,
It soon will clear. Don't have a fear
    Of what the sky portends,
If cloudlets start to break apart
    And leave a patch perchance—
Enough of blue a-coming through
    To make a Dutchman pants.

This adage old and oft retold
    May vary race by race,
But age to youth conveys the truth
    Of what clears outer space.
The weather-wise with all their tries
    Can't beat an upward glance
At just enough of azure stuff
    To make a Dutchman pants.

FOR PEACE

Oh, Lord, we pray that tensions cease;
That this, our world, find lasting peace;
That all suspicion, greed and fear
May quickly, wholly disappear.

We ask, when we must surely know
Our efforts have "a way to go";
That we must show a change of heart,
But, Father, help us get a start.

Reveal Your will—Your holy plan—
For one big brotherhood of man.
Help those succeed who'd truly be
At peace with men—at peace with Thee.

PERSPECTIVE

It's all right here
    For the world to find.
No man's a seer.
    Some are just less blind
To their small phase
    Of surrounding earth
And earn our praise
    For outstanding worth.

The atom's power—
    The whole blasted bit—
Foresaw the hour
    When it would be split.
Beneath the seas
    Ores of wealth wait still
And tempt and tease
    Man to dive and drill.

The moon we share
    In the sky above
Has been up there
    Since the days of love.
Our air supply
    And our water too
I didn't buy.
    Did they come from you?

Yet we go on
    Like we owned the place
When most we've done
    Is to take up space.
A few reveal
    Or make wonders clear;
But none conceal
    Who has put them here.

HIS FIRST PIN-UP

He came home from the party
    quite pleased with himself.
His hands and his pockets
    were loaded with pelf—
With nutcup and sweets
    and a yellow balloon:
All proof he'd experienced
    a big afternoon.

His features, complete
    with a pink paper cap,
Conformed to the lines
    on felicity's map.
He'd partied before
    yet 'twas diff'rent today.
The secret was found
    in a big box of clay.

The clay, he explained,
    As we stood overawed,
Was his for a deed
    that we had to applaud—
A deed generations
    have hastened to hail:
He'd pinned on the donkey
    that fugitive tail.

A PIONEER PORTRAIT

A grandma of mine
    Spoke in quaintest ways;
But now I incline
    To repeat some phrase
Like this, I have kept
    For the truth it lends:
"We have to accept
    What the good Lord sends."

Her life wasn't one
    That was blessed with ease,
But 'til it was done
    she would answer pleas
Of those as they wept
    O'er what grief transcends,
"We have to accept
    What the good Lord sends."

A stoical sort
    Who portrayed an age
That took its support
    From the Bible page,
Whose faith never slept
    But sustained its ends:
"We have to accept
    What the good Lord sends."

A POET'S PRAYER

Give me a page that's clean and white.
    Give me a pencil sharp.
Give me a thought that's good to write.
    Make of my mind a harp.
Help me to tune its strings to sound
    Notes that are sweet and true.
Help me to feel what thought I've found
    Comes through the grace of You.

Teach me to play the proper words,
    Those that delight the ear,
Those that will sing like lettered birds
    Paused on a paper sphere.
Lend me the rhythm of wind and sea
    Sent through a surging soul.
Lend me the will 'til the hand of me
    Fashions its pencilled whole.

Answer me then what each poet's dared
    Ask in his mortal span—
Answer my longing to have it shared,
    Shared with some fellow man.
Heaven forbid that I pray it climb
    Up to the realm of art.
God, I'll be grateful if it in time
    Warms but another heart.

PONDERINGS

Did she, His mother, reminisce . . .
And did it go a bit like this?
"Just as my time was 'bout to be,
My husband said, by some decree
We had to go . . . so he'd been told . . .
To Bethlehem to be enrolled.
It was a dirty, weary ride,
And Joseph walked it by my side.
When we arrived 'mong all his kin,
There was no lodging at the inn.
But in compassion someone gave
Directions to a little cave,
And in that shelter so forlorn
My little baby boy was born.

So sweet and gentle right from birth!
And yet I knew He'd change the earth!
I had been told He was God's Son,
And, as His life was just begun,
Above us shone a holy star
That drew three wisemen from afar.
From hills nearby the shepherds came
And called my baby by His name.
They said that angels had appeared
And calmed the ones who plainly feared
By telling them of peace . . . good will:
A prophesy that He'd fulfill.
All this had set my child apart.
These things I've pondered in my heart.

PRAYER FOR POSTERITY

Dear God,

Help our youngsters be proud
    Of the land of their birth.
Help them praise it aloud
    Ever stressing its worth.
Help them look for its good—
    All that's rich from the past.
Help them feel, as they should,
    That it's theirs to hold fast.

Help our children accept
    In their lives what is new,
Being sure they have kept
    Proven precepts in view
To apply and to test
    That by which to abide.
Should they wonder what's best,
    Help them, God, to decide.

PROMISE OF PARADISE

If I had lived back
    On that yesterday
When Jesus was slain by sin;
If I'd had the choice
    Of the role I'd play,
I know who I wish I'd been.

Not Caesar, the great,
    Most esteemed and proud,
Whom mobs gave their laud and cheers,
For Christ heard the praise
    Of a craven crowd
Corrode into jumbled jeers.

Not Pilate, who yielded
    His weight to whim,
Not Judas with his disgrace,
Not Peter, who thrice
    In denying Him,
Was scanned by the Master's face.

I wouldn't be these
    Or the many more
Recorded in bas-relief.
If given a choice
    Of the roles of yore,
I'd choose the repentant thief.

WITH A PRAYER

With a prayer in one's heart
Is a mighty good start
    In beginning the journey
        of Lent.
With a prayer unto Him
For whom life held no whim—
    Just a mission for which
        He was sent.

With a prayer let us ask
For His strength in our task,
    For the Carpenter's arm
        as our own.
With a prayer let us sight
What He saw as the right
    Though beholding it
        sadly alone.

With a prayer let us feel
What is good—what is real,
    And reject what is
        shameful and sham.
With a prayer let's recall
His advice to us all
    And the promise of
        God's holy Lamb.

With a prayer let us fill
Our own lives with God's will
    As did He as He sought
        to prepare
For the problems ahead
Which He, too, faced with dread,
    But found easier met
        with a prayer.

PURPOSE

The mountains are for majesty . . .
　　The brooks and birds for song.
The seasons show the cycle
　　To which we all belong.
The rainbow is the promise
　　Beyond the tears of grief.
The Word—the Book—The Bible:
　　The buttress for belief.

The stars are lights for guiding
　　Our commerce and our souls . . .
And lifting up the spirit
　　To loftiness of goals.
All things God gave a purpose,
　　A destiny divine;
So I must search in earnest
　　Til I've discovered mine.

Proverbs 16-4

158

PURSUIT

"Pursuit of happiness" is all
        Our forebears guaranteed.
They didn't make a promise tall
        Or pledge we would succeed.
They let each one elect his goal
        And how and where and when
He'd follow up his chosen role.
        They put no more in pen.

True happiness is never caught.
        Elusive is the chase.
But, often, while it's being sought,
        One meets it face to face.
It may be just a fleeting glance—
        A pause to wink at you,
And yet of this you have no chance,
        Unless you do pursue.

THE RAINBOW

The evidence is ever clear
That God is always very near.
Today I couldn't see His jet.
I searched the sky above and yet
I knew He'd passed. He'd left His mark:
A perfect, unpolluted arc.

THE BLUEST RIBBON

The great reward for those who toil
To summon beauty from the soil
And spread its grace that all may know
The Source from which its blessings flow
Is inner beauty—true and whole—
As though He autographs the soul.

REAFFIRMATION

Who whispers to the willow tree
    To summon it to bud?
Who calls and wakens sleeping seeds
    In springtime's sticky mud?
Who'd even guess that they were there?
    No one with mortal eye!
'Tis He who taps the speckled egg
    And bids the fledgling fly.

Who asks the ivy vines to climb
    And send out verdant shoots?
Who turns to green a grisly lawn
    By rousing up its roots?
Who brings us closer to the sun
    To melt each brook and lake?
'Tis He who warms the heart of man.
    Of that make no mistake!

Who knocks upon the closed cocoon
    The rose bush gently swings
To tell the cozy butterfly
    It's time to use her wings?
'Tis He who's watched this rolling sphere
    Since life was first begun;
Who knows how nature reaffirms
    "His Will on earth be done".

REACH OUT

He's with you, dear. He's standing near.
Reach out your heart and feel
The robe whose hem helped all of them
Who trusted it to heal.

He also cried because one died
He loved in Bethany;
But in that hour He had a power
Denied to you and me.

He knows the cost of feeling lost,
Of being hurt inside;
For wasn't He of Galilee
Himself three times denied?

He knows that shame and loss of name
Aren't simple to ignore,
But His advice should still suffice,
"Go thou, and sin no more."

He's close at hand. He'll understand.
He'll listen to your prayer.
Oh, have no fear. He's with you dear.
Reach out and find Him there.

FOR REASSURANCE

Dear Lord, I've slackened in my pace
To wonder if I have Your grace.
I'm putting thoughts of me aside:
My pettiness, my foolish pride.
All disappointment and all grief
I lay before You in belief.

As You look down You're sure to find
A soul confused—a muddled mind—
A heart unstrung—a cluttered day:
All need alignment to Your way.
Oh, Lord, allow me to rejoice:
Oh, let me hear Your "still small voice".

1 Kings 19:12—Where it tells that God
was not in the wind or
the earthquake or the
fire, but "after the fire
a still small voice"
which Elijah heard.

REMEMBER

Remember is a parlor game
    When played by two or more.
Those most proficient in its aim
    Add years in keeping score.

A common board—a single track—
    Is what the players share.
A toss of talk, and all go back
    To times they can compare.

Remember can be played by one—
    A solitaire of sorts,
But then it lacks a bit the fun
    Of most competing sports.

THE RIGHT ANSWER

A giant check-mark, southward bound,
    Has crossed the sunset sky;
A feathered fork with honking sound
    Has solemnly passed by,
As though a teacher, left of hand,
    Had caught some grave mistake—
Not born of earth, you understand,
    But such as clouds can make.
The question we cannot detect.
    The answer we can't scoff.
It may be just that Someone checked
    Another summer off.

THE RIGHT CONNECTION

I saw a toddling youngster
    Reach up for Daddy's hand.
He didn't watch his fingers.
    He trusted they would land
Within the grip of caring,
    Inside the palm of love.
He made the right connection
    Without a glance above.

We, too, can find our Father
    By lifting up our thought.
Poor aim won't miss the target.
    Our meaning will be caught;
And we'll be quickly steadied
    And guided by His care.
We'll make the right connection
    If we reach up in prayer.

ROOM ON TOP

Oh, the world of competition
    Is a pretty strange affair
For you can't go into business
    Without finding others there.
Every venture's overcrowded;
    But for that you cannot stop
'Cause no matter what your project
    There is room for you on top.

It may take a while to get there,
    For ascension over night
To the realm of which you're dreaming
    Is a rarely scheduled flight.
If you're working on arriving,
    There's no reason you should flop.
Just take hold and keep on climbing
    Toward that room for you on top.

All the scenes keep ever shifting,
    And the faces come and go
In the field of each endeavor
    For a Power planned it so.
And if you can have the courage
    To let fear of failure drop,
You can scale your life's ambition
    To the room for you on top.

SALUTE!

Salute the stars that draw the mind,
The blue of peace and right,
The red of courage, raw, refined,
The purity of white;
The blend of heaven and of earth:
The symbol freedom flies
Above a nation blessed with worth—
Beneath its Father's eyes.

SCHOOL'S FIRST DAY

Some bluster in with surface pride
That covers qualms deep down inside.
Some hang to mom with quivering knees
And give her skirt a death-like squeeze.
Some greet the change with downright sobs,
Decrying how this moment robs
The future of the past's great joys:
The playpen, crib, and box of toys.
This day in every mortal's span
Becomes a "giant step for man".

SEASON OF FIRE

This is the season of fire.
Autumn is burning the land.
Everything seems to conspire,
Keeping it brilliantly fanned.
Sumac is flaunting its flame,
Daring the woods to ignite.
Goldenrod brags of its name,
Lending the roadside its light.

Smoke from the dawn's heady haze,
Smoldering all the night through,
Lifts from the heat of the blaze,
Leaving the essence of blue.
Beauty, in dazzling attire,
Bids all us earthlings behold,
Warming our thoughts by the fire,
Ere it's the season of cold.

SEPTEMBER

Under the heat of the summer sun
The days evaporate.
Quickly they dry up, one by one,
At such alarming rate
All that is left is a spider spun
And verbs to conjugate.

SEPTEMBER'S "SCENE"

September's sorry summer's gone.
She's crying bitter tears—
Much like a child who's hanging on
When time for napping nears.
Old Momma Earth, who's seen it all,
So clearly understands
Because this happens every Fall
Across her many lands.

She only waits beside the crib
'Til Septy settles down
And drops her chin against her bib,
Relaxing some her frown.
Then Momma takes the patchwork spread
That each October weaves
And tucks her in—up to her head—
Then tiptoes out and leaves.

SHINE YOUR LIGHT

Every soul who lives
    Has a spark divine—
One the Father gives.
    It's a light to shine.
It's a talent rare.
    It's a special seed
Meant to grow and share
    In a world of need.

No one else on earth
    Has your private gift
To enhance life's worth
    Or give man a lift.
If your light's not shown,
    Count the endless cost!
Since it's yours alone,
    It's forever lost.

Matthew 5:14-16

SNOW

Once more King Winter's court awakes,
And fairies take to tatting flakes,
    Each one—his own design.
These little tufts so deftly made
Become the royal stock in trade:
    A product super fine.

When all the patterns are turned in,
A whining sound is heard begin,
    As every shape's combined
To make a cloak the Wind may wear
And swirl and flap and fin'lly share
    By leaving it behind.

THE SOLITARY OAK

In yonder meadow's midst it stands
And o'er the field a view commands—
This foreman rooted to the soil
To oversee the farmer's toil.
No other trees are growing near
To share its joy or grief or fear.
It stands a lonely oak.

The branches on its western flank
Are shorter for the wind can spank
A tree that has no leafy friend
Against these blows to help defend,
But otherwise the sun and storm
Have fortified its massive form.
It stands a sturdy oak.

It didn't choose this spot to grow.
Some quirk of nature left it so.
Within its grain it may regret
Its station, but it doesn't fret.
Instead it feeds the squirrels and birds
And lends its shade to swelt'ring herds.
It stands a useful oak.

SOMEONE

All of us need a real someone who cares,
Someone who watches our daily affairs,
Someone with faith in the things that we do,
Hoping in earnest our dreams will come true—
Hurt when we're hurt by unkindnesses done,
Happy to share in our moments of fun—
Someone to lean on when sorrows arise,
Someone we know will sincerely advise.

All of us need a real someone to hear
Words not entrusted to everyone's ear,
Someone to tell us we're doing alright
Just when we're 'bout to relinquish the fight,
Someone with patience that love only knows,
Steadfast no matter what fortune bestows.
Surely, we're blessed by the workings of fate
If we can feel that that someone's our mate.

THE SON OF GOD

When the temple was torn,
And the rocks upward borne
   With the shudder of quaking sod,
The centurion said
Of the Lord who was dead,
   "He was truly the Son of God"

He who gave these words breath
Had watched others as death
   Took its toll in its own good time.
'Twas his job to be hard
And to have scant regard
   For the sinners who paid for crime.

But This Crucified Man
He was ordered to scan
   Had a power compelling belief.
Who but God's loving Son
With His life nearly done
   Would give Paradise hopes to a thief?

"It is finished", he heard,
And it must have occurred
   To this Roman beholding God's Son,
If his heathen heart knew,
That the future would view
   What was "finished" as barely begun.

HERE'S TO SPRING

Here's to little twigs a-bobbin'
As they catch a flitting robin
      And then toss him on again.
Here's to warmth and its returning
As though earth were truly yearning
      For a love affair with men.

Here's to all awaking creatures
With their multi-varied features
      Now so busy—claw and wing.
Here's to green, the great transfusion,
Proving faith is no illusion.
      Here's to wonder! Here's to spring!

SPRING TONIC

In the springtime we burst
    The cocoon we call "home"
With a hunger and thirst
    To explore and to roam
In the very same way
    That the moth feels an urge
To be gladsome and gay
    And from wraps to emerge!

There's a something that sings
    In the heart of each one
Who beholds growing things
    Stretching forth to the sun.
Both the forest and field
    Give mankind a real thrill
When new life is unsealed
    By Divinity's will.

Verdant liquid seems poured
    Into branches and leaves
As the holy reward
    Faithful nature receives.
And this tonic is spilled
    In the veins of each man
For his spirit is filled
    With the truth of God's plan.

A SPRINGTIME PRAYER

Oh, Lord of Spring in soil and air,
Grant me a life more full and fair
    By putting springtime there.

Grant me a mind that opens up
Like petals of the buttercup
    To see, to sense, to sup.

In me put power to push and grow
Unhampered by the cold and snow—
    Past winter's wind and woe.

Give me a heart by spring renewed
And fed 'til fertile with the food
    Of love and gratitude.

Implant my soul with strength of seed
That works with wisdom 'gainst the weed
    To fill some human need.

Please oil my every spoken word
With what You use to "song" the bird
    So I'll be sweeter heard.

Oh, Lord, to balance what is rife
With self concern and senseless strife,
    Put springtime in my life.

IN THE STILLNESS

In the stillness, Oh, Lord,
 Hear my suppliant prayer.
As my heart is outpoured,
 Let me know You are there.
This, my season, is dark.
 I am weak and afraid.
Lend my being a spark
 So my faith will not fade.

In the stillness somehow
 I feel closer to You—
Feel You're listening now,
 Understanding me, too;
That You know pain and grief—
 Since all living began—
Shake a mortal's belief
 'Cause he's only a man.

In the stillness, reply
 To my soul and my mind,
Explaining the "why"
 I would earnestly find;
But, if that can't be done,
 Help me see it Your way.
In the name of Your Son,
 In the stillness, I pray.

179

FOR STRENGTH

Oh, God, I ask Your pardon
    For weakness that You see
As, kneeling in the garden
    Of my own Gethsemane,
I ask the cup be taken—
    Your plan for me undone;
In much the mood forsaken
    Experienced by Your Son.

Give me the strength I'm needing
    To bear what lies ahead,
That I, when done with pleading,
    May say what Jesus said:
"My soul so filled with sorrow,
    So heavy as You see,
Will trust unto the morrow
    Your Will—not mine—for me."

STRETCH MY FAITH

Lord, stretch my faith to cover
    All dark and flitting doubt
Where'er it seeks to hover
    And toss its shade about.

Oh, stretch it 'til I'm willing
    To rest upon Your arms,
Though earthly days be chilling
    And nights sound strange alarms.

And let me feel I'm growing
    The while my faith expands
Like glass that's formed by blowing
    And shaped by Unseen Hands.

Oh, stretch my faith. Oh, stretch it
    To serve mankind and Thee,
Assured the more You stretch it,
    The stronger it will be!

Hebrews 11:1-3

SUMMER NIGHT

Walk yourself 'neath the dome
    Of a summer night's sky.
Let your reasoning roam.
      Soul—stretch! If you try,
You can hear and compare
    With the sounds on this sod
How "the heavens declare
    The glory of God."

SUNSET

A giant glob—an orange ball—
    Drops slowly to the lake;
Then in the blue proceeds to fall,
    But leaves within its wake
A sky so smeared with brilliant hues
    One may presume the saints
Have let the little cherubs use
    The mix for finger paints.

SYMBOLS

Mankind in all its length of lore
Has searched for symbols to adore,
    But never could a Tsar,
A Pharoah, Caesar, prince or king
Presume to match with anything
    A Baby and a Star.

A ruler's crest, a coat of arms,
Was one of man's inspiring charms
    When knighthood knew no bar.
Today the flag we love so much
Flies high but still can never touch
    A Baby and a Star.

While all their earthly days are spent,
Most folks are trophy-scepter bent.
    For vict'ry signs they spar.
Yet when their mortal marks are made
For all of them they wouldn't trade
    A Baby and a Star.

The symbols man for man erects
Are such that he in time detects
    How temporal they are
And how they fade when they're compared
With those Our God in Heaven bared—
    A Baby and a Star.

TENANTS

If you close the door on Virtue
    And refuse to let her in;
If you drown her gentle knocking
    With an overriding din;
If you lock and bar the windows
    And draw down the blackened blind,
She may take the hint and leave you
    With your emptiness of mind.

If you laugh because she's folksy
    And old-fashioned in her way,
Or because her dress is homespun
    And she always seems to say
What is "square" and never "with it,"
    She'll reluctantly depart
Taking with her what has furnished
    The interior of your heart,

When she's gone, you'll get new tenants,
    For a vacuum is abhorred.
Will the premises be cared for?
    Will they pay their room and board?
If they don't, and you evict them
    From what then's become a shack,
There's scant likelihood that Virtue
    Will be willing to move back.

MY THANKS FOR OTHERS

Oh, Lord, how very much I owe
To others whom You've let me know
    And see from day to day—
The young, the old, the in-between
Who make an entrance in the scene
    In which I'm called to play.

Another's sweet, approving smile
Can make my efforts seem worth while
    And crown my will to try.
Encouragement another speaks
Is oft the spur my spirit seeks
    Though not quite knowing why.

And, yes, I'm even grateful too
For those who have a dimmer view
    Of me and my poor part
Because they challenge me to test
What's truly noble, pure and best
    Within my mind and heart.

I often wonder how I'd be
Without the folks surrounding me—
    My vital, living hem.
That's why I pause to give this prayer
To You it pleased to put them there.
    I thank You, Lord, for them.

THANKSGIVING

Let's look at the shelves
    of our daily life.
Just back of the jars
    filled with toil and strife
In rows neatly labeled
    we're sure to find
A good many blessings
    For heart and mind.

The harvest is in,
    the preserving done.
All sealed are the fruits
    of the summer sun.
They'll nourish the body
    another year—
Sustain it for purposes
    yet unclear.

It's time to remember
    from whence it came,
Accepting our plentitude
    in His name,
To study the larder
    and then to start
Removing the lid
    from a thankful heart.

THE THANKFUL WAY

God, help us live the thankful way
    In spite of somber strife.
Oh, make us mindful on this day
    That You have given life—
The life that has more good than ill,
    More hope than dark despair,
More kindly warmth than bitter chill,
    More happiness than care.

The thankful way can find the plus
    In all we must endure—
From that which plagues and sorrows us,
    It can distil the pure—
The patience born of failing health,
    The smile washed clean by tears,
The blessings richer far than wealth,
    The love displacing fears.

The thankful way—true praise of God—
    Was felt in Pilgrim hearts
For harvest gathered from the sod
    And faith that it imparts.
May we who share far greater gain
    Too feel the thankful way
And make that feeling very plain
    On this Thanksgiving Day.

THANKING THEE

I thank thee, Father,
    Lord of heaven,
For life and all that
    gives it leaven:
Fresh mornings with the
    chance to do,
Good tasks and strength
    to see them through,
And pride in off'ring
    them to You.

I thank thee, Father,
    Lord of earth,
For showing me the
    Way of worth,
For love and beauty
    'long the road,
For faith that makes
    a lighter load,
And leads to joy
    in Your abode.

THERE AND HERE

When I visit homes so perfect—
    Where no children growing up
Race and run so really rampant
    With their friendly, frisky pup,
There I see the cleanest windows.
    There no smears or marks repose
From two sets of sticky fingers
    And a cold and juicy nose.

There I know the tidy housewife
    Needn't work as hard as I.
When she washes up those casements,
    They will stay the way they dry.
She won't find two minutes later
    What on windows only grows
From two sets of sticky fingers
    And a cold and juicy nose.

Here to polish glass is useless,
    Though I keep the pretext up.
Here the jam and peanut butter
    Look outdoors beside their pup.
Here I pay the greater labor
    For the greater joy one knows
From two sets of sticky fingers
    And a cold and juicy nose.

THERE'S A HUNGER

There's a hunger for the wholesome
    'Neath our violence and strife.
There's a longing for fulfillment
    Of the valued things of life.
There is just beneath the surface
    Virtues waiting to be found,
And there still are lots of people
    With a will for breaking ground.

There's a hunger that is needing
    What's more nourishing than food.
There's an appetite that's craving
    What would change our very mood.
There's no sustenance in hatred—
    No nutrition found in gore.
Having tasted such, folks hunger
    For the things that succor more.

There's a hunger to be moral—
    To be fed by faith and worth,
To be filled with love and justice
    And to taste the good of earth.
There's a hunger for the wholesome.
    I am sure, for if I'm wrong,
What we've cherished as a nation
    Won't be with us very long.

THOUGHT

Man by thought can blend his colors
   Til his life's a work of art;
For he is, the Bible tells us,
   "As he thinketh in his heart".

He can take the red of courage
   And the verdant shade of growth
And so tinge them with his thinking
   That his soul absorbs them both.

He can take devotion's whiteness
   And sincerity's clean blue,
And by thinking so affix them
   They determine what he'll do.

He can take the bitter blackness
   Of one thought that's truly mean,
And his day—perhaps his lifetime—
   Will be muddied and unclean.

Use of oils in every color
   By experience is taught,
And man has for his selection
   All the varied tubes of thought.

As he chooses, life develops
   As a blotch or thing of art,
For man is, and there's no doubting,
   "As he thinketh in his heart".

THREADING OUR WAY

Each day's a bead we thread on string,
A bauble or a golden thing.
    Sometimes we think we choose
From Time's big box held over head
The kind we want, then find instead
    It was a day to lose.

When we don't reach, a bead just falls;
And oft that one the heart recalls
    Had loveliness to bring.
With years come beads of every hue,
And we are grateful for them, too . . .
    And for our length of string.

THREE WISHES

If some small fairy said to me
    (As I have heard they do),
"Of all life's wishes, you pick three,
    And I'll make them come true."
'Twould not be easy to select,
    But one I'm certain of—
Some folks whose love I could detect
    And some whom I might love.

Then, I believe, that I would choose
    An understanding heart—
An inner salve that I could use
    When projects fall apart,
An ointment that I might apply
    When suffering from pride,
A medicine to make me try
    To see the other side.

A faith would be my final choice—
    A faith so real and warm
I'd feel its glow when I rejoice
    And when I face the storm.
Three wishes surely aren't enough,
    As any sprite can see,
But wouldn't life be pretty rough
    If she denied these three?

TIME TO RETURN

Come back to the stable,
    Ye world of men.
Come back to the story
    Of Christ again.
You've wandered. You're weary.
    You know you are.
Come back to the wonder.
    Behold the star!

Your lot is a struggle.
    The ends don't meet.
You work and you worry
    To stay defeat.
You're bothered with problems—
    With pain—with fear.
Solutions escape you
    Or won't appear.

For such is the venture
    That men call "life",
And faith in a Power
    Beyond its strife
Is still the best solace:
    The proffered rod.
Come back! It is Christmas.
    Come back to God.

THE TIMELESS WAY

Today I walk with sages,
　　With saints and serfs and kings,
With martyrs down the ages.
　　I walk as though on wings.
In mood of celebration
　　I join the pressing throng
As part of every nation
　　Seems pushing me along.

The weak and strong are melded
　　To make a mighty mass
That moves like water welded
　　In waves that will not pass
But wash me o'er tradition,
　　'Bove history and lore
Toward what this expedition
　　Is really looking for.

All share the joyful motion . . .
　　The little children dance . . .
As 'cross this peopled ocean
　　On every side I glance.
I know as I'm proceeding
　　That You're with me and them
Because the way is leading
　　Through time to Bethlehem.

TODAY

Yesterday's a shadow,
　　Made of memories now past,
Most of which should be forgotten.
　　Very few will ever last.

And tomorrow is a shadow,
　　Is a dream of things to come.
Some are dreaded, some are hoped for,
　　In our vision of its sum.

Ever try to hold a shadow,
　　Or to stomp upon its shape,
Or to chase it back and forward
　　While it made its weird escape?

One can't hurt or heal a shadow
　　For a shadow cannot feel;
But today is not a shadow.
　　No, today is very real.

TODAY WE'RE FREE

Today we're free to think, to plow,
　　To build, invent, explore—
Pursue the clues to why and how
　　Of life and all Its lore.

Today we're free to try and fail;
　　To struggle and succeed,
To let the best in each prevail
　　To fill another's need.

Today we're free because men gave,
　　On penalty of death,
A sacred pledge to bind the brave
　　And give this nation breath.

Today we're free without a doubt!
　　May He whose charge we be
Let every morrow raise the shout:
　　"Thank God, Today we're free!"

TONSIL TICKLER

By the fairies he was banished—
    By the good ones and the bad—
And from sight forever vanished
    O'er a habit that he had.

He just couldn't sit and listen
    While another sounded off.
With his impish eyes a-glisten,
    He would let a rasping cough.

Though he begged for lighter sentence
    From those fairies in the know,
He declined to show repentence;
    So it meant he had to go.

"I'll be gone, but let me labor
    In the meeting rooms of men,
Setting man against his neighbor
    With a good cough now and then."

"I'll be gone," he kept on pleading,
    "But just let me tickle throats
While the ministers are reading
    Sunday's choicest Bible quotes."

"Let me start a chain reaction
    During music or a play
At the height of the attraction,
    And from you I'll stay away."

So the fairy board relented,
    And it granted him a quill
Which the many he's tormented
    Know that he is using still.

Though they blame it on the weather,
    It's that naughty little elf
Who, by tickling with his feather,
    Makes a nuisance of himself.

TWILIGHT

The twilight is a lovely time
    To let one's fancy roam.
The sun's day shift is then complete,
    And he is trudging home.
Those pinkish clouds with golden rims
    Are footprints where he's trod
Upon the blueness of the sky,
    The pathway known to God.

As yet the night has not arrived
    To take the watchman's round.
But nature knows he's on his way
    And hushes every sound.
The footprints fade and grow obscure
    As darkness drains their hues,
And all God's creatures settle down
    To take another snooze.

TWO SCOOPS

I didn't see it happen—
    this, oh, so sad event.
I don't know where the victim
    in deep dejection went.
I only know the ice cream
    that once had filled a cone
Was lying on the sidewalk,
    a-melting and alone.

A tongue had hardly licked it.
    How perfect yet its shape!
I fancied him who'd lost it
    and mourned its swift escape.
Who'd learned how fate can topple
    near triumph from its throne
And leave anticipation
    with just an empty cone.

TWO TRAVELING SALESMEN

Last night old Febby packed his bag.
    We thought he'd never go.
His yearly visit is a drag.
    He manufactures snow;
And he's the agent for his wares
    From Oregon to Maine.
The samples he so freely shares
    Give most of us a pain.

This morning, ere the room was cleaned,
    March carried in his case—
Brochures from which it may be gleaned
    He means to own the place.
A shamrock fell—a kite tale flowed—
    From what we saw him bring.
We only hope he can unload
    A dandy brand of spring.

UNDER THE TREE

Under the tree on Christmas Day,
Ribboned in colors rich and gay,
Sit the surprises bought and made
Waiting the hour of loving trade.

Under the tree the random stack
Lies as it fell from Santa's pack.
Each little gift will play its part.
Each is to please a child at heart.

Under the tree 'tis plain to scan
All of the time it took to plan
What would delight and furnish cheer
So's to make merry this time of year.

Under the tree we share the joy
Born with the birth of one small Boy,
Born and reborn in God's design
Under the tree—the faithful pine.

VACATION TIME

From the mountains folks are pouring
    For a visit to the plains,
From the cities they're exploring
    In the mountainous terrains.

They are rushing by the legion
    North and south and east and west,
Each to see the other's region
    At a wanderlust's behest.

They are golfing, fishing, hiking.
    They're in ships and cars and planes.
They are swimming, dancing, biking.
    They're in motor boats and trains.

They're the folks across the nation
    Oh, so tired, as they'll attest,
That they needed a vacation
    Just to get a little rest.

VALENTINE'S DAY

Caught in a climate
    so callous and cold,
Born of a bearing
    benumbing and bold,
There is a pause
    that defies winter's way
Known unto people
    as Valentine's Day.

Not in the summer
    when weather is warm,
Not in the season
    that's senseless to storm,
Not when the birds and
    the blooms are their best—
No, it arrives when the
    days are distressed.

This is symbolic:
    a heart where it shows,
Melting for others
    their mantle of snows,
Giving life's ribs
    an affectionate shove.
Such is the soul
    and the substance of love.

VISITING OURS

A nasty old cold laid our Bobby low,
And all he could do was just sniff and blow.
Confined to his bed with a fevered brow,
Our boy was quite lonely, as you'll allow.
So Daddy invited his pals at play
To peak in the window and try to say
A word that would hearten his ailing boy
And bring him a measure of cheer and joy.

He hoisted them up for a look through the screen,
And each said "Hello" like a punched machine.
Though Bob seemed delighted to tell them all
Details of his illness, they seemed to fall
Like rain from a duck, as the adage goes,
For out on the lawn a debate arose.
As each one was lowered to solid ground,
He entered the discourse in tones profound.

The first one recalled just how sick he'd been
When measles attacked him with spotted skin.
The second was moved to remember mumps
And both of her painful and swollen lumps.
A third was reminded and so retold
The troubles she'd had from a far worse cold.
Out there in the yard one could have his pick
Of solace that usually soothes the sick.

WALKING WITH SOMEONE

The thermometer reading
    Was right above eight
When our girl left the house
    At a speeded-up gait
So's to join with a friend
    Who was just going by.
When I warned of the cold,
    I received a reply
Rather wise for a child
    Not eleven years old,
"When you're walking with
      someone,
    It isn't so cold!"

She, of course, never thought
    That philosophy dwelt
In the answer that simply
    Revealed how she felt;
But I'm certain you know
    It's eternally so.
When the winds of defeat
    And discouragement blow,
There's great warmth in just
    having
    A hand you can hold.
"When you're walking with
      someone,
    It isn't so cold!"

THE WAY

In Joseph's tomb
    On Easter morn,
The dark of doom,
    The sin, the scorn,
Were left beside
    The winding sheet
To there abide
    With death's defeat.

The stone was moved
    Some time that night.
The angel proved
    That Christ was right.
His life fulfilled
    What prophets said;
And, as God willed,
    He'd gone ahead.

It's hard to part
    With any friend.
Where does one start?
    How does one mend?
To soothe, to ease,
    What can one say?
Christ answered these,
    "I am the Way."

A WEDDING

Hope brings its heart to a wedding.
Trust bears its soul with a ring.
Strong are two strands met for threading
Life and the goals it will bring . . .
Knotted together believing
God smiles His best from above,
Watching their wedding start weaving
Their special pattern of love.

A WEDDING PRAYER

Dear Lord, we look to You and pray
Upon this very special day
    When two we love are wed.
We look to You with grateful hearts
As joyfully their journey starts
    With vows they both have said.

Dear Lord, please give the best in life
Unto this husband and this wife,
    And help their home to be
A fount of faith, a port of cheer,
A haven free from fret and fear—
    A pride to them and Thee.

Dear Lord, our love is ever strong,
But now they each to each belong
    In love that's fused anew.
Oh, give its flame a constant glow
And warmth that always lets them know
    That they are loved by You.

WHAT'S NEW

Tell me what's new about Christmas?
  Tell me what's new about love?
Is there a more modern manger?
  Is there no starlight above?

Tell me what's new in the story?
  Didn't the wisemen arrive?
Didn't the shepherds see glory
  Stream from the heavens alive?

Hate, have you found a new Herod?
  Greed, have you found a new inn?
World, have you found a new savior
  Willing to shoulder your sin?

Man, have you altered the message
  As through the ages you've trod?
Tell me what's new about Christmas?
  Tell me what's new about God?

WHOSE GARDEN?

I own a garden.
    I plant and I hoe,
But I've a partner
    I think you might know.
He mixes seasons
    And ripens my seeds.
For His own reasons
    He adds a few weeds.
He gives me sunshine
    And showers and soil,
Sparks my ambition
    And ardor to toil,
Smiles at my pride in
    The things I have grown
And when I speak of
    The garden "I" own.

A WIDOW'S EMPATHY

You who've lost and sob with grief—
Loosened even from belief—
Cry, I bid you! Let it out!
From your inmost being shout
How you hurt in flesh and bone,
Ravaged, broken, left alone.
No one really cares or shares
In the depths of your affairs.
No one can! You know life's worst.
Now to no one are you "first".
Need and purpose down the drain!
Never have you felt such pain!
Wounded, crushed, bereft of love!
Through your tears ask Him above,
"Why hast Thou forsaken me?"
Then, and only then, you'll see
Meaning in your earthly role.
God will whisper to your soul.

A WIDOW'S TRIBUTE

Don't raise a monument of grief
    For him who's gone ahead,
But build a firm and fast belief
    In what the Master said.
A heart who's loved you all his life
    And shared the lot you've had
Would hate to have his faithful wife
    Be sorrowful and sad.

Don't write an epitaph of tears
    Because it doesn't suit
A man who, as he strode his years,
    Collected joy en route—
Who always sought the sunny side
    And seemed to find it too.
You know, when dark clouds were your guide,
    He told you they were blue.

Don't make a marker that conceals
    The good that he has done,
But fashion it so it reveals
    His virtues . . . every one.
The finest tribute you can give
    Is just to take an oath
To live the life he'd have you live,
    And live it for you both.

213

A WINTER BLESSING

Though the season, Lord, is winter
   With its sullen sky and storm,
We are gathered where the shelter
   And the friendly hearts are warm.

It's for this we pause to thank You,
   We who know that spring will come
And the earth will bloom with flowers,
   Though right now it's cold and numb.

For this faith we're ever grateful,
   As we are for food You give.
Bless them both that we be strengthened
   For the way You'd have us live.

                Amen

WINTER MORNING

The sun wakes later but is seen
With greater glory for no green
   (Except the needled pine),
Can shade the eye that fills the east
Or dim its brilliance in the least
   As it looks into mine.

Its glance upon the land I know
Sows glitter on fresh-laden snow;
   Then adds an overlay
Of shadowed patterns as the breeze
Bestirs the barren arms of trees
   To lift a winter day.

WINTER SYMPHONY

Upon a staff of frigid air
Drop notes of quiet flakes . . .
A solemn score for all to share
Until the tempo breaks.
Then branches of the soundless trees,
As though directed from afar,
Swirl great crescendos on a breeze
That's muted as a star.
The sharps and flats are scampered tracks
Sketched quickly 'cross the snow
To add a tone that heaven lacks . . .
Played pianissimo.

WITH LOVE

With love you each now enter
    The life you hold most dear,
And there you vow to center
    Your best from now and here.

With love the pledge is spoken
    That sends you forth as "we".
With love you give a token
    Of love eternally.

As one, two lives are heightened
    Beyond the dreaming of—
And all life's tasks are lightened
    When done by two—with love!

Genesis 2:24

WORTH-WHILE PRAYER

Oh, help us keep the things worth-while,
    The things that we've been taught,
The things for which in spite of trial
    Our founding fathers fought;
The things for which a Washington
    Rejected crown and throne;
The things that have by grace and gun
    Been made our very own.

Oh, help us keep the right to choose
    The leaders of this land
And never by indiff'rence lose
    What makes her good and grand—
Her boundless vistas for man's dreams,
    Her fenceless faiths and creeds,
Her spirit bursting at its seams
    To fill her people's needs.

Oh, help us keep our courage dry,
    Our loyalty aglow,
Our sense of justice ever high
    That all the world may know
How sure we are the way is best
    That others may defile
Because we are the living test
    Of what is most worth-while.

216

WRONG WORRY

Next door to me there is a tree
Resounding well with noise.
It has to bear a crop that's rare.
It's growing climbing boys.

The human shoot is coy and cute
A-swinging limb to limb,
Inciting fear from over here
Of one small falling "him".

Young legs and arms give living charms,
I'm sure you will agree.
If I'd be wise, I'd empathize
With that arthritic tree.